BEING BETTER *Than* Your BEST

How You Can Raise
Your Own Bar
By Recreating
Who You
Really Are

DANNY AND MARIE LENA

BEING
BETTER *Than*
Your BEST

Published by
Possibility Press

Manufactured in the United States of America

Acknowledgment

We acknowledge and dedicate this book to our many wonderful teachers who gave us powerful examples. Special thanks to our three Mikes—Michael C. Rann, Mike Matoin, and Michael Komechak.

Thank you to all those special people who have contributed messages and stories.

To the many very important and often famous people who took time to be interviewed by us and offered great insight into raising our bar.

To the countless participants in our workshops and seminars—by being open and telling us your stories and challenges. You have helped to inspire us to find the answers we offer in this book.

To all of our martial arts teachers who truly raised the bar—challenging us physically and mentally to be better than our best.

To calm Deb Manning who helped whip the book into shape prior to submission to Possibility Press.

To the staff at Possibility Press for their creative and insightful contributions to the book and their commitment to making it the best it can be.

To our families for their love, support, and encouragement.

To our friends, colleagues, and advocates who have allowed us to shine.

To William G. Phillips for always being there when we need him…we are eternally grateful.

All of you may never know how much you have contributed to our lives! Thank you.

You are all very special.

Contents

Who Can Benefit From This Book?...and How?

This book can help you improve your personal, professional, and business relationships by being *better than your best!*

If you are seeking to advance to a higher position or level of achievement—or simply desiring to be more respected and appreciated by your coworkers, associates, and leaders—this book will redefine the way you approach your business or profession and help you discover how others view your performance.

If you are an executive or leader desiring to elevate your performance level and that of your team or associates, this book will give you new ideas about motivation, persistence, effectiveness, and efficiency. By recognizing key factors, you can help your support staff and associates raise their level of creativity and productivity as well as your own.

If you sell a product or service, or present an opportunity, the SELL Formula and the 90/10 Formula will help you overcome objections and encourage you to press on. Learn how to create and retain positive, valuable, business relationships that help sell you to others.

If you are a manager, you will learn to solve conflicts, reduce negativity, resolve the home/work struggle, and reach goals with easy-to-follow formulas and techniques.

If you are self-employed, full or part time, you will gain boldness and fortitude, and elevate your business to a higher level. You'll discover how to promote yourself and present your ideas, avoid procrastination, stick to a timeline, and overcome obstacles to reach your goals.

If you are a coach or athlete, you will raise your own bar, helping to bring out your team's potential by playing with inspiration, not desperation. You'll learn how to solve internal problems and persist until you succeed.

If you are a student, you will learn to overcome the fear of being who you really are. You'll learn not to worry about what others may think of you. You will discover how to excel by using your natural talents and abilities. You'll be prepared to make a difference in the world!

If you are a teacher, you will learn tools to motivate yourself and your students. You'll be able to avoid burnout and look forward to every day of teaching—like you may have when you first started!

If you are starting over and looking to recreate yourself, this book will help you deal with the past and move on with a fresh start. You'll learn to be comfortable with who you really are. You'll discover how to achieve what you have always desired, including improved relationships and even have more self-confidence!

Why wait? Start now!

Keep the words of John Wooden in mind, "Success is peace of mind in knowing you did your best."

Introduction

Do you ever wonder if you're using yourself to your full potential? Do you sometimes come away from a workday thinking, "I could have done a little better, or worked a little harder?" Did you ever wonder what could happen if you really gave everything your very best shot?

We did too, and it made us wonder, "What is our best and how do we know when we're performing at our best?" Your best is always changing, but you can constantly strive to be better than you were the last time...better than the time you thought you were at your best. This is called "raising the bar."

Normally associated with high jumpers, raising the bar refers to lifting the high bar so that athletes can challenge themselves to jump a little higher—just a little—to endeavor to beat their last attempt. It encourages them to do better than before...not a monumental amount, mind you...just an inch or so. Every time athletes attempt to go a little higher, they literally have to recreate themselves. They have to rethink who they are. They then base their new goals, not on past attempts, but on new perceptions formed by thinking differently about themselves. Thinking this way keeps things interesting, while keeping the athletes motivated. The end result is a sense of accomplishment in knowing that they gave it their best shot. But what if you could do that for yourself?

Think about what could happen if you raised the bar in your thoughts, words, and actions. How much more productive could you be at your job or business? How much more could you contribute to your team or organization? How much further could you advance? Could you produce a higher quality product? Could you give better service? Could your sales and marketing presentations be more powerful?

This book is for anyone desiring to raise his or her own bar, whether it's at the office, at home running a business, or in relationships with colleagues, coworkers, bosses, employees, associates, clients, customers, students, or family and friends.

Chapter One
What *Is* Your Best?

"Always do your best.
What you plant now, you will harvest later."
Og Mandino

There are many books that tell us how to manage better, be more productive, think "outside the box," make more money, and get more clients or associates—even how to "crush" the competition. The very title *Being Better Than Your Best* suggests competition with yourself; in this case, for you to win, while no one else loses. In fact, other people will win too.

When you have something great to offer people, there's always room for you in the marketplace, so competing with *yourself* is truly the key to being your best.

If you're not happy or not finding joy in your work or business, then everything you accomplish will simply leave you feeling empty. That's why some people who basically have all the things they want—cars, money, stock options, retirement plans, pensions, vacations, and so forth—one day look in the mirror and say, "There's something missing."

It's true that aspiring for the things money can buy can be a driving force in our productive efforts. After all, having excess money certainly makes things easier. It's great not to have to worry about paying the bills or buying something for your family or yourself. But a feeling of challenge and stimulation while earning that money is a key ingredient to a happy, fulfilled life. It's

9

wonderful to have a sense of purpose and be fine-tuning and expanding yourself, so that at the end of the day you can say, "That was the greatest version of myself today." When you can say that, it'll be easier asking the boss for a raise, going to the next level in your business or profession, asking a client for the order, taking on that next associate, being bold enough to speak up at a meeting to offer your ideas and vision, or courageously pursuing new prospects. What a feeling of empowerment!

Being better than your best immediately leads to the question "What *is* your best?" You may have thought that your best was graduating from college after a high school teacher told you that you weren't college material. Or perhaps your best was surviving a layoff and starting and building your own successful business…or becoming a skilled speaker after overcoming a childhood stutter. Your current best may be attaining a high position in a firm that didn't hire minorities 20 years ago! The gauge on your best changes at different times of your life as you continue to grow and become better than your best.

So how can you be better than your best when you may not even know what your best is yet? By raising your own bar you create a new model to aim for—a higher standard, where your new vision of yourself is your role model! You can do this with any of your goals or dreams…whether you want to increase the success of your own business, seek to rise to a higher position within your company, or simply desire to be more appreciated, respected, and motivated in your job or business.

To raise your own bar you must step outside yourself, face your fears, and challenge yourself to not only *think* outside the box, but to *live* outside the box. You need to apply all the principles you have learned in all the motivational, team-building, and you-can-do-it-too conventions, seminars, and training sessions you've attended. You need to not only intellectualize those ideas but take action on them as well—do what they suggest doing! That's living outside the box. That's making it real. That's being the best you can be! Remember, as Albert Einstein said, "You cannot change your current conditions with the same thinking that created those conditions."

Chapter Two
Recreate Yourself

*"Everyone who got
where he is had to begin
where he was."*
Robert Louis Stevenson

To redefine and recreate who you are takes attitudinal and behavioral changes. And the emphasis is on you. The great news is you can start right now! Why wait? You don't need anything to start but a dream or a goal and the desire to grow to new heights!

Before you can recreate yourself, though, it's important for you to understand how you have created yourself up to this point. Who you are didn't just happen. You've shaped and defined yourself in a number of ways—through your *Thoughts* about yourself, the *Words* you've spoken about yourself to others, and the *Actions* you've taken to support how you've described yourself.

The words you use to describe yourself and your life are important. The following story about Jay shows just how important your words can be.

Jay's Word of the Day

When I was a young boy I would often stop at the candy store a block from my junior high. It was a small mom-and-pop place where Jay and his wife worked together. Every time I stopped in I would enthusiastically ask, "Hey, Jay, how are you today?" or "Jay, how's business?" Occasionally, in my attempts to be grown-up, I would venture, "Jay, how's the wife?" One day I asked him a question that started an interaction that continued for my entire eighth grade year.

By chance, one day I overheard my dad say to someone, "What's the word?" I liked that! The next time I went to see Jay to get some sweets, I asked, "Hey, Jay, what's the word?"

After a long pause, Jay answered, "Successful." He stood, waiting for my next move. I was shocked! I was not ready for a one-word answer. It knocked me back a step, so I asked, "What do you mean?"

Smiling, with a twinkle in his eye, Jay replied, "That will be the word for today. Successful means getting what you are looking for in life." So, with that thought, off I went.

The next day I left for school early and stopped at the candy store. Jay was ready with a new word! Enthusiastically he prompted me to ask again, "What's the word?" Even more enthusiastically, he answered, "Together!"

Jay said that each day we would *be* our word of the day. Then he asked me, "How would you act today if you were 'together'?"

"I guess I wouldn't let anyone upset me."

"You've got it! Every day we'll have a new word. Then we'll go out and be that word for that day."

I learned from Jay that defining who you are is simply a choice.

What's *Your* Word?

What if you were asked to define who you are? What words would you use to define yourself? What if you started using positive, empowering, and inspirational words when talking to everyone?

By changing the words you use to describe yourself, you begin the most amazing change on the inside and out...you begin to re-create your life.

Go to a dictionary every day, and find an uplifting word—your "theme word for the day." Then effectively be what that word means throughout that day.

Now think about how you define yourself...what word or words would you use? Your words are important!

T W A—*Thoughts, Words, Actions*

What you are experiencing at work or in your business is a direct result of your daily *thoughts*, *words*, and *actions*. How many of your thoughts are positive and energizing? How many words do you speak that are encouraging and uplifting? How many of your actions are constructive?

By your daily, hourly, and minute-to-minute choices, your life can be either boring or outstanding; just another day at work or a miraculous gift; self-defeating or personally empowering; a painful, uphill struggle or a gentle, steady, positive progression. Our thoughts, words, actions, and the experiences we have as a result of them ultimately create either a vicious, negative cycle or a positive, creative circle—whatever we choose, whenever we choose. What's *your* choice?

T N T—*Totally New Thinking*

As Ralph Waldo Emerson said, "Life consists in what a man is thinking of all day." Emerson stated it so simply, but *do* we actually create all the circumstances and situations in our lives by first thinking about them?

Research indicates that we have around 60,000 thoughts a day. Everything starts with a thought. The invention of the computer, the wheel, and the printing press all began with a thought. It was the collective thoughts of many that created the space shuttle, the Empire State Building, and the light bulb. We have created many things, great and small—enhanced digital television, the Internet, snow shovels.

Someone had to use Totally New Thinking to improve on many of these bests. Along with new thinking, they had to follow it up with new words and actions, which led to the new and familiar experiences we enjoy today.

I Believe I Can Fly

Two brothers watched a bird soaring, and they thought about how wonderful it would be if man could fly. Talking about this dream filled their days and nights. They consulted with other dreamers, technicians, experts, and craftsmen. They began to build their dream, eventually making it a reality.

On December 17, 1903, they experienced four short flights at Kitty Hawk, North Carolina. The mode of transportation we take for granted today began first as a spark of thought in the Wright brothers' minds. They believed manned flight was possible and that they could make it happen.

Everything that is created—be it a discovery, invention, event, or something tangible or intangible—has one thing in common. We refer to it as the Creative Circle, and you're already living it. And now you're going to learn to recognize it while you're doing it.

You can use the Creative Circle to have experiences you desire and create situations and developments that are ideal for your personal growth.

Your personal growth has an effect on others. Small changes in you can create big changes in the world, especially your own. Change your thinking and you change your life! You can even have the joy of helping others change theirs, too, and really make a difference.

Always keep in mind what Dwight D. Eisenhower, former president of the United States, said: "Freedom has its life in the hearts, the actions, the spirit of men and so it must be daily earned and refreshed—else like a flower cut from its life-giving roots, it will wither and die."

Chapter Three
The Creative Circle

"Events, circumstances, and such,
have their origin in ourselves. They spring
from seeds which we have sown."
Henry David Thoreau

The Creative Circle is quite simple. Our thoughts lead to our words. (There are, of course, other ways to communicate besides words. However, for simplicity, we'll refer to the primary, not necessarily the most effective, form of communication as our words.) Our words lead to the actions we take and the outcome of our thoughts, words, and actions becomes our experience.

The Creative Circle concept can be applied to any experience. Start thinking positive thoughts, speaking positive words, and taking positive actions. By doing this you will create a new reality—a new experience of life as you know it.

Being better than your best means different things to different people. Perhaps you simply want to be happier. To accomplish this, think happy thoughts about yourself and your situation. Actively and consciously think happy thoughts about others; look for the best in people. Speak happier words about your life and your current circumstances, using the words, "I'm so happy about that!" Speak optimistically about the world.

Then, *act* like a happy person—smile more, walk more briskly. Be lighter on your feet. Laugh more. Refuse to engage in negative conversation or gossip. Expect great things to happen.

Then, when they do, acknowledge them by saying, "Of course!" Instead of being blasé about life, be excited and enthused—even about the little things. You will then have the experience known as "being happier."

As a happy person, you will realize that even if a sad or unfortunate experience happens, the big blow will only be temporary. As Abe Lincoln said, "This, too, shall pass." Happy people look for the best in every situation. Even if a challenge presents itself long-term, happy people find the good in it rather than staying in self-pity. They may find a cause to rally for or another creative way to do what they want to do.

Maybe you desire greater success. Again, it's time to raise your own bar! How? Think successful thoughts, speak the words that a successful person would speak, and act like a successful person would act. Celebrate even the smallest victories. Congratulate yourself by saying, "I am happy with myself. I feel great about what I have accomplished." Make a habit of congratulating others on their successes too—that's what confident, successful people do. The outcome will definitely be one of success for you.

If your experience is not what you envisioned, then, as a successful person, you know there is no such thing as failure. There are only outcomes. Everything is meant to be a learning experience. Acts that you initially viewed as failures are really successes—you learned how *not* to do something. It is possible to make "perfect" mistakes, because sometimes we need to know what we *don't* want to happen so we can recognize what we *do* want to happen.

Using TWA (thoughts, words, actions) in this way, you will "ooze" with success. Everyone who comes in contact with you will notice. People will begin to treat you as if you are successful. You'll believe it, and you will achieve it!

As Frank Lloyd Wright observed, "The thing always happens that you really believe in; and the belief in a thing makes it happen."

Right now, your inner-critic might be thinking: "Just a minute! I've heard all this 'positive thinking, believe-and-achieve' stuff before." Hearing it is one thing, but actually putting it into action is quite another. Remember, it's challenging to remember what you've heard, and easier to remember what you've seen. But when you actually do begin something, that's when you'll start to understand!

With TWA you now have a step-by-step formula—keys to unlock any self-imposed restraints or barriers to your success and happiness. You know you can't change the past, but you can look forward to the future by changing your attitude whenever necessary.

Even if you have a fear of the unknown, jump in with both feet! Logically you know that your thoughts, words, and actions create your experience. Now, choose the experience you desire and make it happen using the Creative Circle.

Raise your own bar by applying these concepts to your job or business:

- Think thoughts of commitment and excellence in your job or business—thoughts of productivity and completion of the activities essential to your achieving your goals and dreams.
- Communicate the importance of doing what needs to be done quickly and as correctly as possible, given the skills and experience of everyone at work or associated with you in your business.
- Take action to lead your team members or associates through your example of due diligence for the task or activity at hand.

When your day has ended, you will know the experience you have just had was worth all you are earning in compensation. One of our own sayings is: "Change is good. You go first! Once you've raised the bar, take a few practice runs at the new height!"

"To feel good about yourself, you need to feel good about your work. No matter what kind of work you do, it needs to be fulfilling and satisfying. And when you decide that WORK means Willing to Offer Resources and Knowledge, you'll realize you're helping others, and it won't seem like work anymore."

—Danny and Marie Lena

Chapter Four

Never WORK Again

*"What a person accomplishes in a day
depends upon the way in which he approaches his tasks. When
we accept tough jobs as a challenge to our ability and wade into them
with joy and enthusiasm, miracles can happen. When we do our work
with a dynamic, conquering spirit, we get things done."*
Arland Gilbert

That's right. Never work again—especially if you define work the way most people do...

> **W**ronged
> **O**verlooked
> **R**ejected, and
> **K**nocked, out!

Why do many of us struggle with work? Why do many people feel mistreated, victimized, unnoticed, disregarded, discarded, beat up, and deadened at the end of a workday? The highest incidence of heart attacks occurs on Monday morning between 7 and 9 a.m. Many people literally go to jobs that kill them!

Charlie McCarthy whimsically noted, "Hard work never killed anybody, but why take a chance?"

People often say, "My job is my work." TNT, Totally New Thinking, gives you a new definition of work. Your job isn't your work. Your work in life is to live happily and leave this world in better condition than when you got here.

19

Most people have a job so they can survive day-to-day. Chances are it's not where their talents lie nor are they doing what they love—or even particularly like. In fact, 70 percent of people hate their jobs. Isn't that sad? They haven't found or even searched for, in many cases, work or a business that they love or even like very much. They may excuse it by saying, "It's a J-O-B." But what kind of life is *that?*

Could you imagine being born with the following life mission: "First get a good education and then find a job. But since it will be something you hate, you had better get involved in a sport or a hobby on the side to fulfill yourself." Hopefully not!

You may be building a home-based business on the side so you can retire from your job. That's great and something to look forward to. But in the meantime, you owe your employer a good day's work every day for the time you're still there. *Katharine Hepburn refreshingly commented, "As for me, prizes are nothing. My prize is my work."* You need to be such a great worker that your boss will be sorry to see you go! Who knows? Maybe he or she will become one of your business associates down the road. It wouldn't be the first time that has happened!

Do You Hate Mondays?

Do you work with people who tick off the days of the week something like this?

First, they whine in a nasally, self-pitying voice, "I hate Mondays...." On Tuesday they complain, "Today feels like a Monday." Wednesday brings, "Augh...middle of the week...hump day." Then, on Thursday they moan, "Oh, man...I can't wait for...

Friday! WHOA! Weekend! Party!"

Then, all too soon, it's back to that nasally whine, "Sunday.... Work tomorrow...."

Unhappy workers seem to do just barely enough so they don't get fired and they get paid just enough so they won't leave. But that certainly doesn't sound like any fun.

Every day people go to jobs they hate. Why? "It pays the bills." Many jobs pay the bills. If you're in a job that pays well, and feel that you cannot even think about leaving, then find something especially enjoyable about that job. Be the best you can be at that particular task. You made an agreement to do the work for the pay you're accepting. After all, it's your choice to work there. No one is forcing you!

If you go through your life hating Mondays, you've committed yourself to hating one-seventh of your life. What a waste. Mondays are inevitable; why not make the best of them?

For starters, change the way you consider Mondays. Wear your brightest colored shirt, blouse, or dress. Wear a tie or scarf that sparkles. Walk into the office and shout, "Good morning! It's Monday! And it's a great day!" Decide not to wake up with the negative news; instead, listen to an inspirational or motivational audiotape or uplifting music. Awaken ten minutes earlier, walk a little more briskly, and smile at everyone. They'll wonder what you are up to!

Redefining WORK

Wouldn't it be nice to enjoy your work and feel excited going there—no matter how soon you might plan to retire? Your work is one way you express yourself—the predominant way for most people. To feel good about yourself, you need to feel good about your work.

Martin Luther King said, "If you're going to sweep streets, sweep streets the way Michelangelo painted pictures."

No matter what kind of work you do, it needs to be fulfilling and satisfying. After all, it's a big part of your *life,* isn't it?

How would your life change if you walked into work tomorrow and decided that WORK meant Willingly Offering Resources and Knowledge? What would happen if you would also apply these attitudes to the business you may be building? It would cause you to really make things happen, wouldn't it?

So, let's take a look at the components of these uplifting, empowering attitudes:

	Willingly	
Freely	Enthusiastically	Cheerfully
Eagerly	Gladly	Voluntarily
Readily	Happily	Generously

Offering

| Presenting | Proposing | Donating |
| Giving | Contributing | Serving |

Resources

Commitment	Resourcefulness	Prospects
Natural advantages	Mentor/leader	Brochures
Skill	Creativity	Manuals
Perseverance	Website	Tapes
Ingenuity	Contacts list	CDs
Books	Videos	CD ROMs
Property and home-based offices	Company or Corporate supplier	

Knowledge

Information	Brochures	CDs
Facts	Manuals	CD ROMs
Data	Books	Training sessions
Practical ability	Videos	Seminars
Continuing education program	Company or Corporate supplier	Conventions

What would happen if you willingly gave away information, generously wanting to help someone else advance or move ahead? What if you shared your skills, ingenuity, and data—even your possessions—with others at work or in your business?

This concept is totally counter to the way most people view work or business. In today's competitive corporate climate, employees often feel threatened by others who know very much. We've actually heard of members on the same technology team who were withholding information about a product they were developing! We know of veteran teachers not sharing simple information with newer teachers because "I had to learn the hard way. Why should I make it easier on her?" It's considered common practice with some speakers or salespeople to not share techniques or client information with others for fear that others will have an advantage over them. This is old, outdated, nonproductive thinking.

How sad to live in that self-centered state of fear! There is nothing to fear about sharing. No one can take away that which you have given. Remember that whatever you give away will come back to you many times over. Be generous.

Tomorrow, at work or in your business, make a conscious effort to volunteer useful information, data, or ideas that you normally wouldn't share. Take an interest in the successes of your employees, coworkers, or associates. Be sincere. Offer it to someone you normally would not share with, saying, "Let me share some information with you that might be helpful."

Watch their reaction. At first it may be one of skepticism. But when they sense you are genuine, they will be pleasantly surprised. You will realize that you had nothing to fear. Notice the multiplied return when, later, other people decide to willingly help you! Once you develop the habit of giving and serving, miracles will happen in your life.

It's Not About You

As much as we may have been led to believe that our work or business and our place in the workplace or business arena is about us, it's not. It's about discovering who we are in relationship to others. It's about a bigger picture. It's about learning, growing, understanding, and creating the best life possible, not only for ourselves, but also for the world around us. When, on a regular basis, you decide to WORK (Willingly Offer your Resources and Knowledge), you will find that you are not only doing things to be better, you are actually being better than your best. It's no coincidence that this book's title, *Being Better Than Your Best*, contains the word *be* three times!

So, never go to work again—that is, work defined the old boring way. When you are open-minded and prepared to willingly offer the best you've got, watch how your work experience will change. As Charles Schwab said, "The man who does not work for the love of work but only for money is not likely to make money nor find much fun in life."

"When you practice identifying areas of struggle, then root out the struggle response and replace it with positive action, little by little, you will free up your life."

—Danny and Marie Lena

Chapter Five
Life Is Not Meant
to Be a Struggle

"The road to happiness lies in two simple principles:
Find what it is that interests you and that you can do well, and
when you find it, put your whole soul into it—every bit of energy
and ambition and natural ability you have."
John D. Rockefeller III

Struggle is "effort laced with emotion and desperation." Many people struggle with balancing homelife, work, a second job, and often a part-time, home-based business. When they're home, they're thinking about projects at work. At work, they're thinking about what they're missing at home—quality time with their children or spouse or things they need to do in their own business.

One simple answer to this dilemma is to make the most of your time no matter where you are. Operate in the present moment and totally experience every experience. Have the attitude, as Henry Ford advised, "There is joy in work...there is no happiness except in the realization that we have accomplished something." For example, here are some dos and don'ts for when you are at work or building your business:

- Start working as soon as you arrive. Make a schedule for your after-hours business activities and stick to it.

- Don't spend time gossiping, whining, or complaining. Be positive and edifying—look for the good in everything and everyone all the time.
- Don't get bogged down with useless, unproductive activities or time wasters.
- Learn to say no to activities that take you off the track to your goals.
- Make a to-do list for each day or record your tasks in your day planner, according to their order of importance.
- Stay focused on what you need to do and do it.

By using a few time-saving techniques, your activity management will be much more effective. You won't be worrying about what you didn't accomplish elsewhere.

When you come home from work, don't bring all the job stress and anguish home with you. Leave it at the office! When you get home, be totally there.

1. Greet your children with open arms.
2. Let the dog jump on you and lick your face!
3. Give your spouse a big hug and kiss. (Do this *before* you let the dog lick your face!)
4. Don't process your day as soon as you get home, and don't gripe at the dinner table. Share only positives while eating, and save any negatives for discussion after dinner.
5. Put the workday behind you. Totally experience your time with your family.
6. Turn off the television.
7. Appreciate mealtime by giving thanks and enjoying your food.
8. Be quiet and listen to your children ramble on about seemingly unimportant things. This will actually help you to unwind. Children don't need to hear you complain about your job or business. That'll teach them that work is something to be dreaded!
9. If you have your own home-based business on the side, discipline yourself. Make calls, go out and meet new people, build your prospect list, share your opportunity, product, or service with others, and attend whatever meetings and seminars you need to attend.

10. When the day is done and you're getting ready to go to bed, look deeply into your spouse's eyes and give thanks that you have had another great day together.
11. Read from a positive book for 15 to 20 minutes.
12. Take five minutes of quiet time before bed to silence your mind. Take five and stay alive!

People constantly ask us, "How do you stay so happy? Are you always like this?"

We, of course, have had our share of unpleasant moments and days. Like you, we find ourselves in situations when things are not what we anticipated. Some things are simply unavoidable. However, we do endeavor to avoid adding more stress and struggle to our lives—like compounding negative situations by reacting or flying off the handle. This is another way we've recreated ourselves. Life's too short to rile yourself up about little things that you'll forget a day or two from now.

Struggling With the Past

No matter what has happened in our lives, we have always found ways to find happiness or some deeper meaning to whatever situation presents itself. We have certainly had our share of negative experiences—the inevitable ups and downs of running our own business; Dan's divorce and being estranged from his children; the subsequent loss of everything we owned; financial challenges, and bankruptcy. Believe us, we're not asking you to do anything we haven't done before!

We've triumphed over the tragedies we encountered in our youth. Dan was molested at age 11, and, at 15, I was kidnapped and violently abused. Even these seriously challenging childhood experiences later (*much* later) brought us happiness because we changed our attitudes. We believe that God thrust us together when I unknowingly walked into Dan's karate studio to take lessons. We became friends, later fell in love, and decided to dedicate our lives to helping people be happier by recreating themselves (as we have)—reminding each of them of their purpose in life.

We discovered, and hope to convey to you, that to be happy and fulfilled in life, you need to look at situations and circumstances in a new way (TNT—Totally New Thinking). Stop struggling with life's experiences. Don't think you just have bad luck every time a painful or challenging situation or circumstance occurs. Stop saying, "Why me?" Stop playing the victim. That just keeps you stuck. Choose to be happy and rise above it.

A wise woman called Granny once told us that, "Everything in life, every experience, has positive intent. Things happen to either motivate you or to protect you." Simply knowing that has changed the way we look at past experiences we once saw as painful or unhappy. If these challenges had not occurred in our lives, we would never have met each other. We would never have become so passionate about our message, and we certainly would not have written this book and had the wonderful opportunity to share with so many people through our workshops and seminars.

As someone once noted, "Life is what happens to you while you're making other plans!"

We meet so many people with stories that are extremely sad. Some dwell on the past by continually retelling the same story that never has a happy ending. Others have stories just as sad, but willingly change their thoughts about their experiences to find the good. These people share their stories from a positive perspective and bounce back better off for the challenges they went though.

You, too, can begin in this moment to rethink your story. What did you gain from that experience? What did you learn about yourself and others? How can you use this knowledge to benefit yourself and others?

Recreate Yourself

Recreating yourself starts with a thought. If there is a past situation at your job or in your business—an argument with a coworker or associate, a run-in with the boss or leader, or a time when you overreacted and never apologized—if it's still something that bothers you and you can do something to change it, go do it! Apologize, ask for forgiveness, and make amends. Do what you need to do, and *move on!* It's about time, don't you agree?

- What if you changed your thinking and realized that being fired from that job you hated, but stayed with for 20 years because of the "benefits," was the greatest opportunity for you to reinvent yourself?

- How would your life change if you no longer identified yourself as stuck where you are because you have to pay the bills?
- What would happen if you changed your thinking about those with low people skills in your organization and viewed them as giving you an opportunity to excel as a leader?
- What if you just decided not to be shy anymore and start acting as if you were outgoing instead?
- What if you choose to be your enthusiastic, fun-loving self and passionately go for your dreams and goals despite any embarrassment? Imagine what you could accomplish and how your talents could make a difference for the people you help!

There is a wise saying that goes, "You can't change your past, but you can let it go." Let go by finding forgiveness in your heart— both for yourself and others. As you forgive, whether it's directly or just mentally, you may increase your understanding of what happened. The past won't change, but understanding it better can help you feel peaceful about it, let go of it, and move on. By making this mental change, you will be amazed how the world around you will change too! You will have a different, higher perspective on everything. Opportunities will occur to help you appreciate and feel happier about all aspects of your life. Your heart will be lighter and you'll be more grateful—even for the little things!

Are You Running Out of Time?
We often fill our lives with maintenance activities that keep us busy but accomplish little more than maintaining the status quo. Remember, we all have just 24 hours a day. It's simply a matter of priorities as to what gets done. To have more time to do other things, delegate non-productive activities—like mowing the lawn, washing the car, cleaning, and other household and property chores—to someone else. Either your kids, the kids in the neighborhood, or someone else could possibly help you.

How much of your day is spent on things that would be in the Top Ten on your priority list? According to W. Somerset Maugham, "The passing moment is all we can be sure of; it is only common sense to extract the utmost from it."

Life is precious. But we can lose sight of that fact if we're in a constant struggle over time. Let go of some of the busyness and learn to say no to status-quo-perpetuating activities. Start to better manage your activities so you can invest your valuable time in your future. Decide what it is you need to be doing toward your next goal and do something about it every day.

The Best Answers Are Often the Simplest

We were always struggling with time; always late for appointments, running through airports, missing planes, even showing up late for speaking engagements. We finally decided we *had* to do something about it. We saw a sign in a restaurant for a "Time-Management Seminar." Just what we needed! (Time management is really a misnomer because you can manage only your activities. Time marches on, no matter what we do or don't do with it.)

The seminar started at 7:30 p.m. and we were late! We showed up at 7:45, huffing and puffing, ready with our excuses for the instructor. "No problem," he said. "It really doesn't start until 8:00. I just put 7:30 on the flyer. It's a time-management seminar. I know everyone's going to be late, so I don't struggle with it anymore!"

We sat in the front row as the speaker began addressing the entire group. He asked, "Who has the biggest problem with time? Raise your hands."

We threw our hands up in the air.

"We do! We do!"

"Tell me about it," he said.

We proceeded to unfold the entire drama to him and the group, adding our usual flair with hands moving, excited voices, and so forth. "We're always late—running through airports, arguing with cab drivers to drive faster, explaining to meetings planners why we're late, getting stuck in traffic!"

Exasperated and looking for sympathy about our harrowing schedule, we asked, "What can we do?"

The instructor looked at us, pointed, and said, "*Leave earlier.* Next question!"

Wow! Those two simple words cost us $350 but changed our lives! TNT! Now we leave earlier, give ourselves plenty of time, and no longer struggle with being late.

The Money Struggler

More often than not money challenges have to do with having too little, or at least thinking you have too little based on your current expenditures. We know well about the struggles people can have with money; we've been there. We used to constantly feel pinched; too much was going out and not enough was coming in.

If you have a lack of money, don't focus on it. Stop talking about it. You'll never have enough, no matter how much money you make, that is, if you're always spending more than you earn! You'll just be broke at a different level. It's that simple. Stop fretting and let go of that struggle.

Concentrate on what you need to do to serve more—to be more productive—as you follow your heart, fulfill your purpose, and live your dream. The money you receive will be a byproduct of what you're contributing to make other people's lives better. If you've been given an opportunity—a vehicle to achieve your goals and dreams—for crying out loud, go for it!

As it says in *Proverbs*, "As you think, so shall you be." Begin thinking affluence. Think first class. Think wealth. Wealth is a result of someone having given more to others as they went along. They earned it. The great thing is that someone can be *you!* Think, say, and do things like a prosperous person would. Would they invest their time wisely? Yes! Be generous. You can always find someone who has less than you. If you don't have money to give away, then be generous with your service—your time invested helping others. Be patient with the process. Remember, it takes a number of years to be an "overnight" success!

The Sick Struggler

Do you know someone who always seems to be sick, or is constantly complaining about coming down with something? You never see them without a tissue wadded up in one hand. They're walking around sneezing and spraying, warning you to keep your distance. If it's not a cold, or hay fever, or walking pneumonia, then they've got sciatica. When that fades away, a knee starts acting up. Then, when the knee improves, they start sniffling and hacking again! They rarely just have a mild cold. They get an exotic flu or virus, or a whopper of a cold.

So much of our attitude is reflected in our physical health. What is the possible benefit to someone who's constantly struggling with sickness? For one thing, they can generally count on the sympathy vote. They also have a ready-made, all-purpose excuse for not doing their best—on the job or in their business—never mind better than their best! How can anyone who behaves like that ever expect to achieve their dreams and goals?

Stop talking about any ailments you may have. You get what you focus on, so focus on being healthy! If someone asks you about your bad knee, say, "I'm working on it and getting better." If you feel the pain there, instead of complaining, say a prayer for help, consult an expert if necessary, and imagine it being healed. With every step you take, think of your knee (or whatever body part it is) getting better and stronger. There are countless stories of ailing people—some with cancer or other serious illnesses—who, because of a positive, hopeful attitude, find their conditions healing. The mind is a powerful tool; make it work *for* you—not against you. Remember, the mind controls the body; the body doesn't control the mind!

The Struggler's So-Called Perks

Since struggle is "effort laced with emotion and desperation," why in the world would anyone choose to participate in it? The problem is, when someone is perceived to be struggling with something, there's a good chance other people will sympathize with them and cut them a certain amount of slack. It seems like the best thing to do. But it's not! It just reinforces where they are.

A struggler says to the world, "I'm hurting. I'm not up to speed. I can't be expected to shoulder my share of the load." Most people sympathize with someone like that because someone else probably sympathized with them in their difficult time. However, strugglers continually invite struggle into their lives and never really want to overcome it. Why? Because it seems to serve them well. It gets them sympathy, attention, and rest. But the problem is it never gets them the better life they *really* want. That's called lowering the bar. Showing them sympathy is like crawling down in the hole with them, which only helps them stay there!

Struggle is really just a substitute for positive action. Effort is being expended in struggling. No one could justly accuse the struggler of not putting in his or her fair share of time and energy. Just look at the mountain of paperwork to be tackled; it never gets finished. Look at the jam-packed schedule. Isn't he or she constantly being paged? Who in the world could possibly ask *more* of the struggler?

If you make an empathetic suggestion that would help the struggler crawl out of the hole, he or she always has a ready-made excuse why it won't work. The struggler slumps into the same heap at the end of each day, exhausted, with precisely no progress made whatsoever. In fact, he or she may even be regressing.

Eliminate Struggle and Move On

Examine your life for any areas where you seem to constantly spin your wheels. What might you continually fret about? Your in-laws? Your job? Your health? Your children? The lack of progress you're making in your business?

Pretend you are your own best friend. Become your own personal witness. What do you hear yourself whine about a little too often, a little too enthusiastically? Do you cover new ground, or are you rehashing the same old issues over and over again? Isn't it all getting rather boring? Aren't you tired of hearing yourself complain? Decide on the positive steps you can take to resolve the struggle and move on to better things.

Since struggle can act as a barrier, putting life on hold for us while we incessantly run in place, facing life without struggle may seem a little scary at first. But when you practice identifying areas of struggle, then root out the struggle response and replace it with positive action, little by little you will free up your life. The thrill that you'll feel over the forward motion will help motivate you to keep the struggle out. You'll gain more and more self-confidence in your ability to overcome challenges.

Being Better Than Your Best

To eliminate struggle, write down these statements and repeat them daily:

- Today I will be the master of my emotions.
- There are no problems in life, only opportunities and solutions.

- If I am not part of the solution, I am part of the problem.
- What I believe, I will receive.

Charles Kingsley recommends to, "Thank God every morning when you get up that you have something to do that day which must be done, whether you like it or not. Being forced to work, and forced to do your best, will breed in you temperance and self-control, diligence and strength of will, cheerfulness and content, and a hundred virtues, which the idle will never know."

Chapter Six

Stay Motivated to Achieve Your Dreams and Goals

"We accept the verdict of the past until the need for change cries out loudly enough to force upon us a choice between the comforts of further inertia and the irksomeness of action."
Louis L'Amour

Gradually, as you reduce and remove struggle from your life, you will find that you have more time on your hands for positive activities—more time to focus on achieving your dreams and goals. Many people with good intentions start out being motivated, but end up falling back into the rut of struggling, which inevitably leads to their losing focus. "How do you stay motivated?" is one of the top ten questions people ask us.

For a time in our lives we were lost, confused, unfocused, and unmotivated. Together we changed our minds one day, saying to each other, "We need to get motivated. This is not healthy...and where are we going if we keep on this way?" We started reading all the information we could on motivation from many different sources—authors, speakers, philosophers, ministers, rabbis, priests, educators, sages, poets, entrepreneurs, humanitarians, athletes, world leaders, luminaries, musicians, and other people we admire.

Now, 20 years later, here is our personal list of the top five ways we stay motivated. Hopefully you will find the *spark* you need in one or all of them.

1. Use your gifts and core talents.
2. Live on purpose.
3. Go for your dreams and goals.
4. Be persistent.
5. Embrace change.

Use Your Gifts and Core Talents

Our talents, capabilities, and gifts are unique. Personal empowerment comes from the intrinsic knowledge that we are doing what we are good at, using our gifts and core talents, and doing what we love—the last being the greatest self-motivator. Ask yourself these questions regarding your gifts and core talents:

- What is my greatest quality, gift, or core talent?
- Where are my talents best suited?
- Am I using my talents and gifts to their fullest?

Have you ever noticed that when you're doing something you really love—when you're following your dreams—everything feels right? Time flies by. Afterward you have the sense of satisfaction that you were really being useful and productive—you were on track. That's being better than your best. You don't rely on external motivation, although that can help. But the main reason you want to keep going is because it feels right. You know you're doing the right thing for you, regardless of what others may say or do.

However, let your efforts truly reflect your abilities—use yourself fully. Exert the effort necessary to fully utilize your many special abilities. We always challenge each other to perform at our best, whether we are working in the office or on stage speaking. We find that we can, and usually do, raise the bar on our own performances. Many times we do even better than we thought we could. And you can do the same. In fact, you can do better too—time and time again! You can pleasantly surprise yourself on a regular basis.

You have probably changed and recreated yourself many times in your life. This time, however, recreate yourself using your core gifts and talents, and let the world see your abilities in action. Allow others to point out your talents, as they often notice them before you do! Give yourself more credit for what you have to offer.

If you're not quite sure what your talents are, or if you're not using them to your greatest ability, make a list of 25 things you like about yourself. Don't be modest! Then expand this list to also include 25 things you are good at doing. It doesn't matter how important they are, or whether someone else would see them as significant or not. Fill up the page!

Now look at all you can do. Look at who you are. Imagine where those core talents and positive qualities could take you in the future. Which gifts would you like to develop? Which qualities do you want to improve upon? What can you do here and now to upgrade yourself...to be better than your best?

You are uniquely special. You embody amazing talents and qualities, whether you believe it or not, that combine to make you unique in the world. Your distinctive talents are tools you will use to change the world for the better. But don't seek to change the world from the outside—those changes are fleeting. Seek to change the world from within. Grow yourself into the person you've always dreamed of being. Real change starts with yourself.

Repeat these positive statements:

"I am changing the world by using my core gifts and talents each and every day. I am making a positive difference."

Live on Purpose

Self-made millionaire and successful entrepreneur Paul J. Meyer says with passion, "My objective is to continue developing and using the skills, talents, and gifts God has given me to make the world a better place."

What is your purpose...your reason for being you? Ask yourself, "Who am I? Where am I? What's next for me?" Indulge in the pleasure of getting to know who you are and what you are good at doing. You have a reason for being alive; be courageous enough to reach, dream, and believe! You have the ability to recreate yourself and begin again—no matter what has transpired in your past. You can raise your own bar on the level of your personal and job or business success. You can be better than you have ever been—better than your best.

Here are some questions to ask yourself regarding your purpose:

- What do I want to accomplish with my life—what are my dreams?
- Is my lifestyle congruent with my values and morals?
- Why do I work where I work, or why am I in the business or profession that I'm in?
- Can I announce my agenda to myself clearly saying why I do what I do?
- What is my purpose in the following areas: my job, profession, or business, as well as my family and community?

If you still aren't sure what your purpose is, ask yourself, "What am I happiest doing? What makes me smile? What things move and inspire me to take action? What do you do that gives you the greatest personal satisfaction and joy? What gets you fired up? What do you do that makes the time just fly by? What do you *really* like to do? What would you do if you had all the time and money in the world?

Your purpose will find you when you follow your inner desires—your heart of hearts. *And just think—what you want, wants you.* It's like a magnet that's ready to attract you.

Your purpose may not necessarily conform to the world's notion of what is grand. Generally speaking, your purpose in life—whatever the specific course may be—is to leave this world in better condition than it was when you got here. That sounds reasonable, doesn't it?

We were presenting a series of workshops out-of-town when, during a break, we decided to power-shop at the department store down the street. During our interaction with the saleslady, her questions and comments came flying at us from across the sparkling glass counter. "Who are you two? You're not from around here, are you? You two are so up! I could use some of your energy. What do you do?"

In unison, our immediate response was, "We help people be better than their best!"

"Oh, motivational speakers—that explains it! Okay, Mr. and Mrs. Motivation...motivate me!"

Without hesitation we asked her, "Do you have children?"

"Yes," she answered. "What does that have to do with anything?"

"Do you have steady employment?"

"Yes, I have a great job. I work with wonderful people; I work for a great company. But how is that supposed to motivate me? I'm tired!"

"You need to get more sleep then. Do your children ever eat?"

"Yes, they eat. But what does that have to do with me getting motivated? I'm having a hard time making financial ends meet."

"You need to spend less, make more, and sell or let go of things that are eating up your money. Do your children need clothes to wear?"

She began to protest. "Yes, but...but! I love my kids...and I get the idea, but you're not motivating me by reminding me about my kids."

Our answer was, "You are looking for your motivation from the wrong source. Your motivation will come from within you. We were just reminding you of your purpose."

Enthusiastically, she said, "Got it! I love my children. I love my job. I get along with my coworkers, and I have a great employer.

"I need a little rest. My financial situation is of my own doing, but I can feed and clothe my kids. Yes, I am motivated; and yes, it does come from within me!"

We finalized the sale, and left with the great feeling of having helped someone.

Your motivation can be found in your purpose. Locate your purpose and focus on it. Then *stay* motivated!

Go for Your Goals

We are goal-setting-and-achieving machines. Our desire to quench our thirst or satisfy our hunger makes us set out for the kitchen. The loose step on the outside porch may mean nothing until someone falls. Then off we go to the hardware store for the brackets, braces, and screws needed to achieve the goal of creating a safe step.

Here are some questions to ask yourself regarding your goals:

- Do I believe that I am worthy and deserve more than my current situation or standing is providing me?

- Do I periodically define my goals and plan their accomplishment?
- Do I have goals that I have written down? Do I read them and refer to them often?
- Do I establish new goals after achieving those I've previously set?
- Do I ever help others achieve their goals without asking for anything in return?

At work, your team's latest project moves you to your computer so you can play your part in the team's success. The addition of an all-new electronic commerce department brings you the opportunity to recreate yourself within the company. You set a goal of learning the new software. You take classes, go to conferences, read books. You watch, learn, listen, and do. Soon that goal is attained.

If you're building a business, your goal of reaching the next level of success motivates you to take part in the continuing education program available to you. For many it includes books, tapes, seminars, and conventions. You have a goal to build a dream home so you consult with someone who is where you want to be in the business you're in, and follow their guidance. Soon you start reaching your dreams and goals—one by one—and you see yourself growing.

Everyone has a goal—even the laziest person! You might ask: "What is the goal of the person with the 'do-nothing' attitude?" The answer is as obvious as the question—doing nothing is their goal, and they're often very good at it!

Some of us have been working on goals from the time we were born. We set out to do one thing; then along the way we lost interest, or moved on in a different direction. We might allow ourselves to be stopped by circumstances seemingly beyond our control, and some of us just plain quit on ourselves. What about you?

Thinking, conceiving, dreaming, setting up plans, and eventually achieving our goals is important to our personal fulfillment and job or business success. Setting up goals and leading a group of people in the direction of achieving them is often essential to business success. Equally as important, however, is the fact that each person needs to have a goal within the company's or organization's overall objectives. Their personal mission will serve as a contributing force to the group's success.

Be Persistent

Unrelenting persistence is the undeniable, unstoppable power, force, and energy needed for any kind of success. But faith is also needed. Have faith in yourself, your family, your country, God, your fellowman and woman, and your current project, goal, or dream. This faith will help you overcome the fear of failure and fuel your persistence.

Here are some questions to ask yourself regarding your persistence:

- Do I quit or give up easily?
- How important is it to me to accomplish what I set out to do?
- What power, force, and energy do I need to draw upon to keep going, especially if it looks as though I'll never achieve my goal?

Now granted, there may be occasional derailments. There might be unavoidable delays, but keep on going! The sweetest successes are usually those that come after many delays and upsets anyway.

There's a fine line between achieving goals and not achieving goals. And it's persistence that usually makes the difference—"stick-to-it-iveness." Sometimes you may anticipate persistence to mean working hard until the end of the week, but your particular goal ends up taking two months—or even two years—of hard (and hopefully smart!) work. However, you will achieve different levels of success along the way. And the greatest gift from all of this is your growth and development. You'll find this to be a priceless prize for your sweat equity that will help you every day in so many ways.

Goal attainment is like priming a pump to get water out of a well. To achieve your goals, you need to prime *your* pump with desire and belief. After it is primed, you need to pump persistently. The water may be one-quarter of the way up or halfway up—you often don't know for sure. In any case, to get water, you must pump. Your success might be just around the corner, but you need to persist before you can see around that corner.

In *The Greatest Salesmen in the World,* Og Mandino wrote, "You were not born into this world in defeat, nor does failure course in your veins." Persistence applies not only to your own goals, but also to lessons you may be endeavoring to teach others you're helping to achieve *their* goals—whatever they may be.

Parents often ask their children, "Do I have to repeat myself a thousand times?" Managers and leaders often ask: "Do we need to always retrain ourselves? Must we constantly refresh and upgrade?" The answer may be yes. It's up to you. You are the teacher and the leader, and the best way to lead is by example. Raise your own bar on persistence to a certain point and you'll attract and help enough people so you can reach your goals.

Professors, coaches, and teachers understand that persistence is nine-tenths of what's required for student success. Too often the only thing that makes one person succeed while someone else fails is that one was committed and persisted until reaching his or her goal, while the other one quit. Patience and maintaining the vision of your goal will help you stay on track.

We have learned in our business that delays are not deadly, and what we may consider failures are not fatal. Life goes on. If you look at things only in terms of success and failure, then you're automatically defining one as the only possible good and the other as purely bad.

Instead, look at a result you weren't necessarily hoping for as just an outcome that doubles as a learning experience. When something doesn't turn out the way you want, ask yourself some questions about the how and why of what you wanted. See this event as an opportunity that points you in a positive direction— perhaps better than the one you were on! Then, too, certain goals, for one reason or another, may not be attainable by you at this particular time. For instance, your timetable may not necessarily be the best for that goal in the overall scheme of things.

As Henry Wadsworth Longfellow said, "The heights by great men reached and kept were not obtained by sudden flight, but they, while their companions slept, were toiling upward in the night."

Now repeat this positive statement:

"Failure is a learning experience and only a temporary detour to my ultimate goal."

Embrace Change

All of life consists of change. Embrace it and look forward to the excitement of the possibilities it could bring. Heraclitus, a teacher of ancient Greek philosophy, said, "You can't step into the same river twice." The water you stepped into will have flowed away by the time you step in again.

To help you embrace change, ask yourself these questions:

- Do I handle change well?
- Do I sometimes resist change? If so, what am I holding onto?
- Am I willing and eager to strive for new things?
- Do I get defensive when I'm faced with change?
- Can I see my negative patterns and am I flexible and committed enough to change to a more positive course?

Change is the way of the world. Nothing ever stays the same because everything is constantly changing over time. Change is also the way of business and of doing business. Over time, the business environment is constantly changing and we need to adapt to it in order to succeed.

There are times when we simply need to make some changes before we can move forward. And change can be a scary thing, so much so that people often continue in an undesirable situation—just because it's familiar and the thought of change and uncertainty is frightening. But if you want some things to change in your life, you need to change some things in your life!

There once was a traveler asking directions from an old man sitting on his porch. At the old man's feet lay a groaning hound dog. The traveler asked, "What's wrong with your dog?" The old man responded, "He's layin' on a nail." "Doesn't it hurt him?" the traveler asked. The old man said, "Yeah, it hurts him." "Then why doesn't he get up?" asked the traveler. The old man replied, "I guess it just doesn't hurt him enough yet!"

What is hurting you now that you could change so you, too, can feel better about yourself and your career or business? How about moving up in your company or organization? That could require a big change. How about increasing your current income level by 25 percent? That's probably going to require a big change. How about doing some positive things to help change the way coworkers, associates, and clients look at you—with new feelings of respect for your kindness and generosity? That might require some big changes. How about treating people so well that vendors, suppliers, and others everywhere you go thank you and tell you it's always a pleasure doing business with you? That could require a big change. How about focusing on how to serve and support others better, thus improving your overall business and personal relationships? That could require a big change.

Here are the three Rs to change:

Initially, you need to: Recognize what needs to change. Look at your behavior—your part in the change situation. Has life thrown some curve balls at you lately? Have you ever asked yourself: "Why me? Why this? Why now?"

We asked ourselves those questions and then realized that what was happening right then provided our greatest chance to prove who and what we were. How? By witnessing our responses to certain situations that occurred, we had the opportunity to change our responses, thereby changing the situations. This is how you actually recreate yourself and various aspects of your life.

Secondly, you need to take: Responsibility. Look inward. Almost all of our challenges are there by our own creation. In many cases, though, outside events or circumstances which we can't control are also involved. However, our *response* to these circumstances is *always* under our control. Look closely at past challenges or negative situations in your life. When were you the "actor"? When were you the "re-actor"?

When attacked from an outside source, did your response come from the best developed part of yourself or from fear and anger? When you were backed into a corner and decisions had to be made, did you use your creative, compassionate and superior-thinking mind? When someone lied and falsely accused you of wrongdoing, did you act or react? Did you forgive and let go?

Our outer actions are an expression of our inner thoughts, desires, and attitudes. What inner thoughts, desires, and attitudes do you need to change?

Finally, you need to: Recognize that change requires taking the right action. It takes courage to look inward and invoke emotions strong enough to take the necessary actions to make a difference in your life. Changing situations and circumstances means we need to make new decisions about who, what, and where we are in life. Then we can go forward and put those decisions into action. Are you ready? (We didn't say raising your bar would be easy!)

The process of choosing what to do next is, for some of us, terrifying. The funny thing is that, as frightened as we may be of making decisions and changes, we are, nonetheless, constantly making decisions and always undergoing change—anyway!

We are all a part of nature, and its components change from one minute to the next. Does the grass get mad when the seasons change? Do insects get flustered and stomp their little feet when the ground is turned over by a shovel? Human beings may get annoyed, upset, angry, confused, and frustrated at the inkling of change. Unfortunately, we may begin resisting it immediately—without even stopping to think about the positives the change could bring.

For some, the hardest part about change isn't change itself, but preparing for change, and setting and maintaining a new course to deal with it. Just consider the absurdity of this example: "Nothing has changed recently in the office. But sometime they may move my desk. Oh no! What will I do then? Just thinking about it makes me think about quitting. Maybe a lawsuit for cruel and unusual punishment is in order!" How absurd is that?

We may resist going with nature's flow. We may turn what is supposed to be a continuous, natural flow into an endless struggle. Life is not meant to be a struggle! But many of us hit the same brick wall over and over again when all we really need to do is take a different action. Turn away from that wall and change direction!

There is a story about a group of condemned villains who were offered a choice. They were told they could face a firing squad or take their chances going through an unopened door, facing the consequences of whatever was beyond it. Guess what. They chose the firing squad! Death was at least a sure thing. In choosing the firing squad, they didn't have to deal with uncertainty.

Unfortunately, they didn't take the chance that freedom would have been behind that door! Is that where *your* freedom lies—beyond the unopened door of a golden opportunity you've been given? Face your own uncertainty and do what you need to do. Otherwise, you'll never know what opportunities you'll lose by your indecision and inaction. You dreams and goals are behind that door—just waiting to be discovered and realized.

A cautionary note: When you do make changes, when you raise your own bar and upgrade who you are, it's possible that not everyone may be comfortable with the new you. Not liking change, some may wish for the old you to return. Don't be swayed off course by others' discomfort with your change. Taking a long, hard look at yourself and changing can be tough, but the rewards you'll gain will be infinite.

Repeat this positive statement:

"I have the courage to look inward and acknowledge the things I need to change." This could include:

- Changing any negative perception of the world I may have; I believe it is inherently good.
- Changing any unkind feelings that I may have toward others I see on a daily basis; I am more tolerant and understanding.
- Changing any negative thoughts I may have about my past; I see past events as valuable learning experiences.
- Changing any stingy attitude I may have toward others; I become more generous.
- Changing any "There's-not-enough" thinking I may have to one of "There's plenty for everyone."
- Changing any fears I may have into joys as I do what's necessary to achieve my goals.
- Changing any unprincipled business practices I may have into ethical habits.
- Changing any deceit and dishonesty I may have into trustworthiness and honesty.

We're not implying that you are necessarily thinking or doing anything negative. But every situation has opportunities for change and improvement. As you become more comfortable making changes, you will be able to forge ahead more easily to improve your life using your gifts and core talents. You will begin living on purpose, moving forward toward cherished goals. You will be more persistent, and you will embrace the changes that life brings—instead of resisting them. You will be motivated! You'll jump out of bed every morning and nothing or no one will be able to stop you!

Now let's focus a little more on your goals and how to make them real and attainable for you.

Seven Super Ways to Make Your Goals Real

Personal, professional, and business goals need to be real or they appear unattainable. Unreachable goals result in discouragement, boredom, and exasperation—even in highly motivated people.

Here are seven ways to make your goals real so you can maximize your possibilities of achieving them:

1. **Be clear:** Paul J. Meyer said, "If you are not making the progress you would like to and are capable of making, it is simply because your goals are not clearly defined." Be specific—down to every detail.
   a. Be *really* specific! Dan and I once decided we would love to go to Paris. It became a very real goal for us. We posted notes everywhere. We repeated over and over, "We're going to Paris."
   b. Shortly, we got a call from a bank president who wanted us to come speak to his staff.
   c. "Could you travel to Paris?" he asked.
   d. "Of course!" we replied, grinning at each other.
   e. "Good," he replied. "It's only a few hours from Chicago." He meant Paris, Illinois!
   f. From that point on, we learned to be *very* specific.
2. **Concentrate on your goal:** Eat, sleep, and drink with your goal! Write it down and look at it several times a day. If it's tangible, take or cut out pictures of it and put them up where you'll see them frequently.
3. **Love your goal:** Love the idea of achieving your goal. Imagine how you will feel when you achieve it.
4. **Make the necessary changes:** Eliminate nonproductive activities. Say no to people or things that redirect you or take you off of your route.

5. **Be persistent:** Be unstoppable…unswayable. This is often the most challenging part. Stay your course, taking the action necessary to follow through. Don't give up.
6. **Be flexible about the outcome:** Many of us have so much difficulty with this! We may always want our goal to be exactly a certain way. Even when we do succeed, we may feel unfulfilled if it isn't precisely the way we rigidly envisioned it. We may fail to realize the importance of getting out of our own way. Be flexible and open-minded about the outcome and allow the goal to come in any form—then, and only then, will you be pleased with your efforts.
7. **Help others achieve their goals:** Lastly, but most importantly, help others reach their goals. Willingly offer all that you have in knowledge, resources, care, and compassion so that you can help others accomplish their goals. Help a child achieve his or her goals. Help your spouse. Help your friends, family, and neighbors. Help your community. Help others you're associated with. Demonstrate to the world that you are a person who can help make more goals a reality that you ever could before. That's raising the bar and recreating who you are!

As English poet, Percy Shelley put it, "The Almighty has given men arms long enough to reach the stars if only they would put them out."

Take a Step Back

Often you will need to step back from your specific goal and look at the big picture. Don't get stuck in the "Why-isn't-this-happening-for-me-now?" attitude. You may have heard the saying, "We make plans and God laughs." Perhaps it may not be the season for you to achieve a particular goal. Maybe a more important goal is in the works for your future…something that you can't currently foresee. Looking back on your life, you'll discover there are often hidden blessings in things that *didn't* happen—things that at a particular time you wanted to happen in the worst possible way but the timing simply wasn't right. Look back on these experiences and accept that timing is key and it will help you to adopt a constructive attitude toward all possible outcomes.

Don't let self-doubt grow until you allow it to prevent you from doing something. People who win stomp out self-doubt by continually raising the bar and growing their self-confidence as they continue to persist.

We've learned that our success in a venture usually lays "just beyond our doubt." If we start to doubt ourselves, we both repeat, "It's just beyond the doubt." When we persist and stay the course, success appears right around the corner! Persistence takes patience. Patience takes willpower. Willpower fuels persistence. And the game goes on. Such fun!

Stop only if you feel there is no purpose anymore to make the effort—that you need to go in a different direction. Otherwise, continue to press on in your desire to succeed! You can do it. You are the best person for the job. We need you. The world needs you. You need you to be better than your best!

Chances are you have never really experienced your best—you probably do not know what you are capable of. So go ahead and test your strengths! Go outside your comfort zone, take risks, and reach for the stars! Look deep inside yourself for the source of strength and will that has been gifted to all of us—the power to think and act. Personal success, the success of the team, and the success of your company, organization, or project are steps away! Be the energetic, enthusiastic spark of light, encouraging others with your upbeat attitude even when the tough times come—and they will come. To be better than your best you need to allow yourself to be used as a tool—the catalyst, the key element—for positive change.

Remember, patience is not only a virtue; it's a required course and habit in the school of life.

Eight Qualities of Persistence

We've written so much about the importance of persistence, but what are its true components? Napoleon Hill's classic self-help book, *Think and Grow Rich*, lists eight qualities of persistence. Incorporate them into your life to recreate yourself:

1. A definite purpose
2. Burning desire
3. Self-reliance
4. A definite plan

5. Accurate knowledge
6. Cooperation
7. Willpower
8. Habit
Here are *our* thoughts on these eight qualities:

A definite purpose—Recognize your purpose for achieving your goal or desire. Ask yourself: "What is my purpose for desiring this goal? Do I want comfort, security, fame, fortune, or something else? When I have achieved my goal, will the world be a better place?"

You might wonder about goals that aren't so lofty. For example, what does losing ten pounds, quitting smoking, having better relationships, or making more money have to do with changing the world? It has everything to do with it! You are going to feel better, work more productively, feel more confident—and you will be a joy to be around!

Say these positive statements:

"My life has a purpose. I have a reason for being alive!"

Burning desire—Burning desire is a white-hot flame of motivation due to intrinsic energy and strength. This internal motivation will push you farther than any outside source of motivation—more than a paycheck, a holiday bonus, a free box of steaks, overtime, or something else external you're offered.

How can you incorporate a burning desire into your quest to be persistent? Wrap your idea, goal, dream, or desired outcome with energy and excitement that gets you up early and keeps you up late. Surround yourself with positive, supportive thoughts and people. Speak only the words of an enthusiastic person on a mission. Ask yourself often, "How great am I going to feel when I have completed my task? When I break through the wire at the end of the finish line, will I have given it all that I have?"

Say this positive statement:

"My desire is the fire that is taking me to the wire!"

Self-reliance—You are the only person responsible for your final outcome. All the classes, all the lessons, all the tapes, books, seminars, and all your life experiences have prepared you for whatever task you choose as an undertaking. Remember...you would not have the desire for a particular 'thing' if you did not believe, somewhere in your mind, that it is possible to acquire or achieve it.

You are the end result of all the experiences and teachers you've had until now. All of your past triumphs will raise you to this point of confidence. So be confident that everything you need you already have.

Say this positive statement:

"I have whatever it takes...and so much more!"

Definite plans—Write down your plans, type them, draw them, or program them into a computer, then think them through. Consult with someone who is where you're aspiring to be as you begin and as you progress. Create a plan of achievement to take you from where you are to where you want to be.

A ship without a rudder will never get to the correct port. A man or woman without a plan is nothing more than a child, lost and afraid who's wandering aimlessly. How will you ever get to where you are going without a map to guide you?

Your plan may not be perfect. It may fail for the particular outcome you desire and may take you in another direction. You may even get lost for a short time—but without a plan you are just spinning your wheels. Address your fears, concerns, and doubts before making your next move. Like an enterprising entrepreneur, do your worrying quickly before you execute your plan. And remember, you have the flexibility to change as needed.

Be prepared to change course if and when an obstacle appears. Take your time, be patient, and work through your thoughts. Consult with your boss, mentor or leader, if necessary. Then, calculate your next move. Now, it's full speed ahead. Go for it!

Say this positive statement:

"I plan my work and I work my plan!"

Accurate knowledge—Do you have the knowledge necessary to achieve your goal or dream? If not, find out what else you need to learn to accomplish it, and take the necessary classes, courses, or workshops. Go to whatever training, seminars, or conventions that are available and that you qualify for. Listen to all the tapes and read all the books recommended for what you seek to do. Observe what those who are where you want to be did to gain their knowledge and duplicate it. Search for the most accurate and up-to-date information possible.

Make your continuing education experiences productive by focusing on gathering all the information imperative to the completion of your goal or project. Ask other successful people in your field for help or advice. You will be pleasantly surprised at how helpful most people are. They will often feel complimented that you asked for their guidance. Surround yourself with knowledgeable people who are willing to work with you. Thank them for their support. Use every source of information possible to you. Then search for more and more and, still yet, more—until you succeed.

Say this positive statement:

"Knowledge is power, it's true; but accurate, usable knowledge is true power and I am acquiring it!"

Cooperation—Learn to get along excellently with people. Be humble and open-minded enough to accept assistance and ideas from others. Be forthright about asking appropriate people for help and generous in offering your help to others with a sincere spirit of cooperation. Yes, some people might take advantage of you. Yes, some will let you down. Yes, you may cooperate and become a team player only to be cut. Your feelings may be stepped on. But for the few people in your life who will take from you, there are hundreds more who will be willing to give back to you. Go for it! You will find the perfect person or team of people necessary for the success of your goal.

Say this positive statement:

"Cooperation is the key to success with others, and I practice it daily!"

Willpower—Think of willpower as self-mastery...knowing who you are and being able to work within that framework...not being afraid to change who you are if who you are is not serving you any longer. Your willpower helps you create a successful attitude because you are constantly changing your idea of success as you grow. Because it's your idea of success and yours alone and you're focusing on it, you become resilient and can bounce back time and time again. You will find, deep within, a power and determination strong enough to overcome any setbacks. The power of your human spirit can triumph over any tragedy or obstacle—it can move mountains.

Say this positive statement:

"I exert my willpower to do whatever it takes to win!"

Habit—Repeat the same thing for 21 days and watch it become a habit. Researchers say three weeks is the average minimum time required to create a new habit, good or bad. Do you want to be better than your best? Start the habit of being more fit. For the next 21 days eat a well-balanced diet, and exercise. If your challenge is smoking, make the decision to quit right now. For the next three weeks say, "No thanks," to friends who say, "Let's go have a smoke." Which of the eight qualities of persistence will you need to help you develop the habit of not smoking cigarettes?

Begin today to realize the importance of every professional or business relationship and personal interaction you have. Your habit of building great relationships will become so much easier.

Say this positive statement:

"I replace old failure habits with new success habits!"

Here is a list of some positive habits which you may want to adopt:

- *Form more productive work habits:* Get to work early, and start working as soon as you arrive. Develop the "and-then-some" attitude—give more than others expect. Become a person others can count on. If you have a business on the side, get right to it as soon as you finish dinner. Use your off-job evening and weekend time wisely to propel yourself to a new level of achievement. Involve your family so you can do it and grow together.
- *Make a habit of doing things you love*: Jog, walk the dog, pet the cat, sew, paint, fly a kite, ride a horse, garden, read a good book, watch a motivational movie, and so forth. These activities are forms of release vital to personal or business and

professional happiness. When you are going for a goal, though, you may need to postpone doing the time-consuming hobby and recreational activities for a while. Then later you'll be able to do more of them.

- *Make it a habit to forgive:* It starts with a choice you make. Forgive faster. Why wait? Do it for yourself. The other person or people are probably oblivious to your resentment and anger. Start now. Create a daily habit of saying "If they would have known better, they would have done better." Ask other people to forgive you faster. Apologize quickly and make amends where needed.

- *Make it a habit to be more loving to yourself and others:* Think loving thoughts, speak loving words, take loving actions. Say, "I love you" faster. Why wait? Start now. Love people even when they disappoint you—love them without condition.

- *Make it a daily habit to be more successful:* Think thoughts of yourself as a success, speak positive, successful words, and take only actions that will lead to your success. Again, associate with success-oriented, uplifting, supportive people.

- *Make it a habit to listen to your heart:* It will give you guidance in decision-making. To do this, pay attention to your "gut" feelings and learn to trust your sense of things. Confidence comes from trusting yourself—your best self.

As Mahatma Ghandi noted, "Keep your words positive. Words become your behaviors. Keep your behaviors positive. Behaviors become your habits. Keep your habits positive. Habits become your values. Keep your values positive. Values become your destiny."

Chapter Seven
The 90/10 Formula

"When you see a problem
coming down the road, holler,
'Hello, Problem! Where have you been?
I've been training for you all my life!'"
Dr. Norman Vincent Peale

You have read about forming positive habits to raise your bar and recreate your destiny. Unfortunately, many of us form destructive habits and exacerbate negative situations. To some extent this is caused by our approach to problem-solving. Most people focus 90 percent of their time on the problem and only 10 percent on the solution.

We are a society of people who are over-stressed and sleep-deprived in a fast-paced, competitive business world. Various policies dictate the way many of us behave and respond to certain situations. Job or business politics may determine the way we handle problems, depending on what the problem is and who it involves.

As a result of all of that, many of the problems we face might be compounded by our reactions and fears about what will happen if we do make a certain decision. We are then left with indecision—leaving us unable to correct the problem.

Most people focus 90 percent of their time on the problem—thinking and talking about it. But this only makes things worse.

With attention, the problem actually grows! This then often leads to drawing other people into the drama, hoping for agreement and support. They argue their position in an attempt to prove they are right. Yet being right rarely solves the problem, and often builds resentment.

Eventually some people even make themselves sick over the problem. They become disgruntled, destroy relationships, and burn bridges. This situation usually results in future cynicism, and the development of a nonproductive, guarded, suspicious personality. How can you be better than your best when your last professional or business experience "left a bad taste in your mouth"? Besides, an unnecessary expenditure of energy is made just coping with this aftermath of negativity.

As English author Jane Austen once said, "Where so many hours have been spent in convincing myself that I am right, is there not some reason to fear I may be wrong?" Are you willing to admit you could be wrong? It could save the day!

Using the 90/10 Formula to Find Solutions

The 90/10 Problem-Solving Formula can help when working with people who have trapped themselves with problems. It can help you solve any problem by seeing it more clearly, so you can better determine the best course of action.

First, in order to solve a problem, you need to look at it straight on and start focusing on solutions. When we go over the problem again and again in our heads, it can take on a life of its own and appear bigger than it really is. It often becomes a swirl of mental activity, much like the gerbil running in a circular wheel, going round and round, huffing and puffing, and surely busy—but going nowhere and certainly not being productive! Here's something you can do to help you be solution-oriented!

1. Create a ten-line document. Draw ten lines across a sheet of paper or in your computer file.
2. On line #1 enter a clear, succinct description of the problem.
3. On the next nine lines enter every possible solution. Then focus 90 percent of your thoughts, words and actions *on the solutions,* without putting limits on them. Think to yourself: *"If there were no boundaries, 'what ifs,' or 'buts,' what could be the solution?"*
4. Start writing.

Your document could look like this…

> **My problem is**:
> 1. _____
>
> **Possible solutions are:**
> 2. _____
> 3. _____
> 4. _____
> 5. _____
> 6. _____
> 7. _____
> 8. _____
> 9. _____
> 10. _____

Now look at your nine solutions and choose the one easiest to implement. Enter it on the first line of a new document.

> **My solution is**:
> 1. _____
>
> **On the next nine lines, enter ways to take action on this solution:**
> 2. _____
> 3. _____
> 4. _____
> 5. _____
> 6. _____
> 7. _____
> 8. _____
> 9. _____
> 10. _____

In doing this, you are putting the "Three Rs to Change" into action as described on page 42.

In stating the problem, you are *recognizing* it. By writing down possible solutions, you're taking *responsibility* for solving the problem.

Thinking of ways to apply these solutions encourages you to take the *right actions*. Some of the solutions you originally wrote down were probably not the right actions for resolving this problem.

For example, imagine that your paper reads like this:

My problem is:

1. A personality conflict with a coworker (or business associate) is creating stress and strain.

Possible solutions are:

2. Write him or her a letter explaining everything that annoys me.
3. Ignore him or her.
4. Talk to my boss, mentor, or leader about it and get help.
5. Be more understanding.
6. Talk to him or her in a compassionate way.
7. Take a look at myself and see how I may be contributing to the problem and stop doing it.
8. Be more open-minded to his or her ideas at meetings and other times.
9. Stop chatting with coworkers, associates, and others about my problem with this person.
10. Learn stress-reducing exercises.

Let's see which of these would be taking the right action.

1. Would writing him or her a letter really solve the problem or would it just add to it? It may add to it because sometimes words on a paper or a computer screen come across as cold and escalate situations rather than resolve them.
2. Is it practical to ignore him or her? Perhaps not. You do need to work together or associate with one another.
3. Talking with your boss, mentor, or leader, who knows you both, may lead to a solution you hadn't thought of. He or she may want to meet with the two of you to work things out.
4. Being more understanding by endeavoring to see things from the other person's perspective would definitely help.
5. Setting up a session with him or her to compassionately discuss your concerns could help. Wait until you have calmed down to do it though!
6. Looking at what you may be doing to contribute to the problem and, of course, stopping it, is always valuable.
7. Being open-minded and not letting your judgment cause conflict at meetings and other times would be effective.
8. Refusing to engage in negative conversation or gossip will help you to stop fueling the conflict. What you give energy to continues.
9. Learning to reduce stress through quiet time or relaxation exercises would help you to deal with the emotions you have about the situation. It'll help you to not take the problem home with you if your job or business is located outside of your home, and would make your time at work or in your business more effective.

Solutions 3, 4, 5, 6, 7, 8, and 9 seem most practical. Agree?

Start with the one you feel would be easiest—perhaps number eight (refusing to gossip about him or her). Then take action! Why wait? Start now. Take care of the matter and move on to other things you need to do to be maximally successful.

As Samuel Johnson once said, "Life affords no greater pleasure than that of surmounting difficulties."

Achieving Goals With the 90/10 Formula
Apply this formula to reach any goal. Remember, there are no limits to the possibilities!

Example #1

My goal is:

1. To become a manager, an executive, or reach another leadership position within a year.

   Possible ways to achieve it are:

2. Observe a manager or leader I admire and emulate his/her positive characteristics.

3. Read books and listen to tapes on managing and leading effectively.

4. Get into the mindset of a manager or leader.

5. Be a problem-solver.

6. Learn to get along well with everyone.

7. Be the person others go to for information and knowledge.

8. Show dedication to my job or business. Get to work or start my business activities early; start working right away making calls or do whatever is most important to do, and make sure that job or business activity gets done.

9. Motivate and lead my coworkers or associates.

10. Ask for the job or share my goal of reaching that level in my business with my leader or mentor!

Never Underestimate the Power of Asking for What You Want

A highly qualified Ph.D. at a large technology firm assumed he was the perfect candidate for an executive level job that opened up on his team. He waited patiently for over two months to be offered the job. His boss instead chose an equally qualified man from the outside to head the team. Shocked and indignant, the Ph.D. demanded, "Why didn't you give me the job? I was perfect for it!" His boss, looking confused, replied, "Yes, you were perfect, but you know I've been looking for someone for over two months. You never asked for the job so I assumed you didn't want it!"

A home-based business owner associated with other independent business owners wanted to reach a certain level in the organization by the end of the year. His goal date came and he hadn't made much progress. Instead, one of his associates walked across the stage and accepted congratulations for reaching the very same level. Disappointed after the event, the first business owner commented to his leader that he had the goal to reach that level too. Surprised, the leader exclaimed, "But you never told me. I would have helped you do it if only you had told me!"

Example #2

My goal is:

1. Increase my business 25 percent.

   Possible ways to achieve it are:

2. Take full advantage of the continuing education program offered by my company, organization, or industry.

3. Follow up with contacts on the phone for one hour or more a day.

4. Send cards and notes to current and previous clients and associates.

5. Associate with and learn from people who are where I want to be.

6. Ask people to hire me or associate with me in my business.

7. Ask clients for referrals.

8. Focus on others and how I can help them achieve their goals and dreams.

9. Keep a positive attitude at all times.

10. Promote myself and my company or opportunity and products or services to everyone.

When the late Princess Diana's visit to Northwestern University in Chicago created such a powerful public interest and media stir, a television reporter asked her, "Out of all the places you could have gone, why did you choose to come to Northwestern University?"

Diana replied, "They asked me."

Noted success expert W. Clement Stone said, "If there is something to gain and nothing to lose by asking, by all means ask!"

Use the 90/10 Principle to solve any problem and achieve any goal. Start with the one solution that is the easiest to implement—then *go!* You need to be free of worry and stress, and encouraged by reaching and attaining your goals! Don't hesitate! Why wait? Start now.

It's failing to start that stops most people from succeeding. Remember what Henry Wadsworth Longfellow said, "Today is the block from which we build."

Timeline vs. Deadline

In the Wild West, criminals were transported on horseback across the plains to go to jail. When the guards would camp for the evening, the criminals would stay within a circled area drawn on the ground with a stick. The guards took turns watching the criminals and if any crossed over that line, they would be shot to death on sight! Hence, the line was known as the "Deadline."

We often describe a scheduled completion date as a deadline. Why not change that to "timeline." Let's face it—you don't want to be dead when you get there!

From our own experience with setting goals, unless we have a timeline, we often allow things to fall by the wayside. We *have* to know when an event needs to be completed. It gives us a track to run on. We also need regular intervals to chart our progress. The goal itself doesn't matter, whether it's writing a book, finishing a proposal, preparing advertising materials, designing and redesigning our web page, or even reaching a goal. Unless we have a completion date, nothing gets done.

Here's a *Six-Week Timeline Chart* we designed for ourselves. It may help you raise your own bar too. You may choose durations of any length...30 days, 100 days, one year. The timeframe is up to you. We work best with six-week intervals.

How to Use the Timeline

- Create a timeline for each and every goal.
- Make several copies and post them where you can see them every day.
- Use your timeline to set up doable intervals within the completion date.
- Mark important dates or milestone events within that timeline to help you stay motivated and on track.
- Fill in the smaller goals accomplished within that six-week timeline to chart your progress.

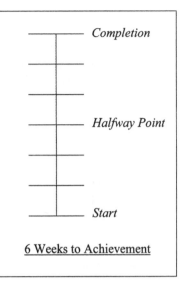

- Watch how much you accomplish in those six weeks!

Look at that timeline every day and ask yourself the following questions:

- What have I done today to put myself closer to achieving my dreams?
- Are my current activities bringing me closer to my goals?
- Are my thoughts, words, and actions each day supporting the completion of my goals?

Now ask yourself: "Is there anything holding me back?"

- Take the time to list anything that is blocking your way.
- List daily activities and note the unnecessary ones that take time but are not relevant to your goals. *Don't mistake motion for action.* There's always "busy work"—which won't move you forward—that you can rationalize by saying, "It needs to be done": things like cleaning, mowing the lawn, miscellaneous

phone calls, and such. We've been there and done that! But it doesn't make any sense.

This is avoidance behavior. Yes, those things do need to be done, but how important are they? Sometimes you can leave the dirty dishes in the sink, or get up an hour earlier, or limit your casual phone call to a friend to two minutes—especially when it means you have more time to work toward your dreams. Sometimes you can delegate chores to your kids, neighbor kids, or others. When you take an inventory of your daily activities, you will find some things you can easily eliminate or delegate to make more time for higher priority activities.

It's all a matter of prioritizing. If your dream or goal is truly important to you, you'll press on and begin doing what is necessary to achieve it—*no matter what!* You'll be amazed at how much you can accomplish in a short amount of time once you're more focused and directed! Once again, don't mistake motion for action!

As Henry Frederic Amiel said, "Conquering any difficulty always gives one a secret joy, for it means pushing back a boundary-line and adding to one's liberty."

Chapter Eight
You Can't Sell It
If You Can't Tell It!

"If the word selling bothers you,
use the word sharing instead—which is really what selling is.
You're sharing something with others to make their
lives better in some way."
Danny and Marie Lena

Tina, our five-pound Maltese puppy-dog knows our backyard very well and relieves herself only within our property lines. However, when she's in heat, she instinctively insists on roaming the neighborhood leaving her scent everywhere. It's the canine version of marketing! How else could male dogs know she's available? She's sharing with them the only way she knows how.

However you choose to express yourself, remember that you need to advertise the idea of a new you—a better you. Although we don't suggest using the same method as Tina uses, becoming a master salesperson is imperative.

Selling Yourself to Others

Good ideas, products, services, and opportunities don't just sell themselves—no matter how much we wish they would! They need to be sold—or advocated—by someone. And other people will get on your bandwagon once they know you care and there's something in it for them!

Don't tell yourself you're not a salesperson—you're *always* selling whether you know it or not. If you have ever been interviewed for a job, written a letter to promote an idea or raise a complaint, tried to sell a tangible or intangible product (anything from a business opportunity to vitamins to insurance to candy bars for your child's team to holding a yard sale), attempted to raise money for a cause, searched for a date or a marriage partner, or simply wanted to have an office holiday party or picnic—you've had to sell yourself and your idea.

If the word selling bothers you, use the word *sharing* instead—which is really what selling is. You're sharing something with others to make their lives better in some way. Then it's up to them what they do with what you're offering.

David Letterman has this advice for guests: "...Whether you're a comedian, an actor, or an author, you're being given seven or eight minutes of network time to come out with your sample case, open it up, and show people why they ought to buy your new miracle sponge. We expect you to come out and entertain.

I'm always amazed at how few people understood that and did it...Steve Martin, Bill Murray. Both these guys always try something new, different, and rewarding.... Even someone like Tom Brokaw.... He understood: 'I'm demonstrating that I'm a reasonable, engaging, entertaining person,' which he is. You're there to show people why they ought to spend seven-and-a-half bucks for your new movie, or watch your show on television. Still, it's stunning to me how many people don't understand it."

Although Letterman is talking about guests on his television show, these lessons apply to almost every situation:

1. Know that you're selling yourself, your idea, product, service, or opportunity.
2. Know that you have a limited time to do it.
3. Entertain, engage, inspire, and motivate your audience, which can be from one person to a whole crowd of people, into taking action.
4. Demonstrate why or how your idea, product, service, or opportunity is different from others.
5. Ask for what you want or want the other person to do. (Stop selling and start closing.)

Good ideas are often thrown out just because of an ineffective presentation. This can temporarily affect your self-esteem. But you can bounce back quickly and continue sharing your ideas or whatever else it is you have to offer. Go through the numbers, as they say, to get the yes or yeses you need.

Remember, if you don't share ideas, they can't be activated. Learning how to inspire and motivate people is an art. Some people seem to know how to sell or share with ease, while for others, this talent seems to be a mystery.

The Gift to Entertain, Engage, Inspire, and Motivate

There is a folktale about a wanderer in ancient times who pulled a magical stone out of his pack, explaining to doubting villagers how the stone could create a wonderful, magical soup. When asked to demonstrate it, the traveler complied with much ceremony, engaging everyone's participation. He suggested that a bunch of carrots and several large onions from the village storehouse would enhance the magical soup. Reluctant volunteers soon cooperated by contributing beans, scraps of meat, and spices. Two strapping young peasants filled the pot with water from the nearby well and hung it over the communal hearth. As the broth began to bubble, a tantalizing aroma filled the air.

The wanderer sniffed the soup, tasted it, and nodded sagely. He reached in with a ladle, removed the stone, and after cooling it, returned it to his pack. Filling large bowls with the delicious soup, everyone ate until their bellies could hold no more. The wanderer departed, leaving behind him a wondrous tale of a magical stone that conjured up the best soup ever.

The moral of the story is offered by the late Mary Kay Ash: "A mediocre idea that generates enthusiasm will go further than a great idea that inspires no one." Surely, if nothing else, the "magical" stone generated enthusiasm!

To make sure what you're offering gets off the ground, follow these guidelines:

1. Develop and implement a sales and marketing plan, with the help of your boss, leader, or mentor, as needed. (If you already have a good one, use it.)

2. Construct and deliver persuasive messages that work in any context. You may need to share what you're offering to different types of people in different environments. Tailor your message to diverse audiences—find out what's important to them, i.e., their dreams, goals, wants, and needs. This will help you have a better idea of how to present your idea, product, service, or opportunity to them in a compelling way. They are interested in what's in it for them, and they'll be watching and listening for that in your presentation.

3. Build and nourish your alliances, networks, and any other contacts you may have. Build bridges by developing and maintaining positive relationships that you develop into friendships, whenever possible, with advocates and others who believe in and support you.

4. Generate loyalty and commitment from colleagues, associates, clients, and contacts. The best way to do this is with passion and commitment, and a plan that people can see is workable and that they can get excited about. If you're selling a product, service, or idea, are you using it yourself? If you're sharing an opportunity, are you running with it yourself—are you being a good example?

5. Seek bosses, mentors, and leaders who have achieved what you want to achieve, and wisely listen to their counsel. Say yes when people want to help you by giving of their time, expertise, or advice based on their experiences. Remember and appreciate them and what they did for you, and, in turn, lead and mentor other people too.

6. Be the most positive, supportive, loving, caring, compassionate, enthusiastic person you can be and teach others how they can do the same.

7. Overcome objections and handle challenging people and situations with dignity. Always honor objections with respect. When people openly object to your ideas, product, service, opportunity, or plan, they may actually be helping you discover mental obstacles. Then you can use the 90/10 Problem Solving Formula to find solutions.

8. Have a Plan B and C. Always have other options you can share with your prospective clients or associates. For example, if you're sharing a business opportunity, there may be someone who is not quite sure about what they want to do.

Your approach may include a chance for people to try out the business by sharing it with family or friends before registering or signing up. They could do this to learn more and meet other successful people.

9. "Think B-I-G!" Don't waste important time on small ideas. Have unlimited vision. Being able to see "the bigger picture" inspires people.

10. Discover ways to present your ideas with P.U.N.C.H:

PASSION—Have energy and show enthusiasm!

UNDERSTANDING—Know and understand your idea, product, service, or opportunity. People want to know that you know what you're talking about or can get them the information they need. If you're not sure of something, maybe because you're new at your job or business, be honest about it and get the answer for them as quickly as you can.

NARRATIVES—Use narratives: stories that create pictures and mental images. People need to not only hear and intellectualize your idea, they need to mentally picture it too.

CLARITY—Be clear and concise. Keep complicated technical talk for the technicians. Explain what you're offering so simply that a ten-year-old could understand it. (But never talk down to your audience—or a ten-year-old for that matter!)

HEART—Involve your heart, your emotions. When your message truly comes from your heart, your sincerity and conviction will be undeniable.

Practice in front of a mirror or on videotape to see, hear, and feel how effective you are.

Go ahead and "Speak the speech, I pray you," as Shakespeare's Hamlet instructed the actors.

Some Speaking DOs and DON'Ts
This is the one area where we see the most challenges. We've witnessed dozens of meetings, presentations, and impromptu speeches

speeches where the speaker has refused to use a readily available microphone. Typical excuses include:

> "I'm afraid of them."
> "I don't need it. I have a loud voice."
> "I'm embarrassed."
> "Everyone can hear me without it."
> "I won't be talking that long."
> "I might blast everyone out of the room!"

If there is an available microphone in the room, *use it!* First of all, using the microphone is not about you. It's about other people hearing you. As you do more presentations, you'll get over any fear you may have of hearing your own voice, and you'll soon learn to enjoy it. Your message and what it can do for your audience is more important than the fear. And don't assume if you have a loud voice that people can hear you. You can never predict how your voice travels (or doesn't), how it dissipates in certain areas, or the general acoustics of the room. We've heard powerful messages fall by the wayside because those in the back of the room simply couldn't hear. We've heard people with the weakest of voices say that they don't need the mike!

Being fearful of the microphone communicates a clear message that you believe what you have to say is really not that significant. We've witnessed presentations at technology seminars where very important technical data and formulas were being explained. One presenter flatly refused to use the microphone, saying that his voice would carry to the 200 attendees. He had a very raspy, high-pitched voice that people were straining to hear. Needless to say, valuable information was misinterpreted and everyone was distracted as they turned to the person next to them and asked, "What did he say?"

We've heard crucial directions doled out to an audience of 300 with the microphone-less presenter prefacing his talk this way: "If anyone fails to fill out the form properly—*exactly* as I dictate—you cannot compete. So, listen up carefully!" People were desperately trying to hear him. That was a setup for failure.

Being afraid of the mike is probably just a result of lack of practice. If you want to be better than your best, go for that mike!

Practice speaking into a microphone. Either rent one or, if possible, practice with the actual mike you'll be using. You will be able to get a feel for its hotness (strength and power). If possible, see if you can adjust the sound levels with the audio person beforehand. This may be the best investment of time you could make to ensure the success of your presentation.

To sell yourself and what you're offering, you need to be able to share it effectively and make sure everyone can hear it. But the microphone will not be your only concern.

Here are some DOs and DON'Ts for a successful presentation:

1. DO visit the room or auditorium beforehand to familiarize yourself with the area. Avoiding surprises will help to eliminate jitters.

2. DO test the microphone. Insist that the audio person turn on the system for testing. Check the sound levels and have him or her make the proper adjustments.

3. DO test the lighting by walking to the most distant point in the room where people will sit. Make sure the audience will be able to see you clearly. If there are dark spots, avoid those areas when presenting. It's very hard to connect with an audience if they can't see your eyes. (It's ideal if you can see them too, but due to glaring lights, especially at conventions, you may not be able to do so. Sometimes, though, you can ask that the audience area be lit, for a short time anyway, so you can see the people.)

4. DO raise and lower the tone and pitch of your voice. A monotone voice will put your audience to sleep no matter how high the volume! Likewise, a nonstop feverish delivery will annoy your audience after awhile, no matter how good the content. Learn to modulate your voice for maximum effect.

5. DON'T neglect any part of the audience. Separate it into quadrants if you need to, and invest time focusing on each one. Speak to everyone in the room. If you can make eye contact in each quadrant, be sure to do so.

6. DON'T put yourself too far away from or above (highstage) the audience, if possible. It can create a lack of communication, and disconnectedness. To better connect, if appropriate, kneel on one knee for a short period or come down off stage for a time and speak at their level. If you plan to venture off

stage, check with your host before your talk, just in case they prefer you not to do so. Be respectful of your host's wishes, and be sure you can take your microphone with you!

7. DON'T mumble! Articulate clearly.

8. DON'T talk too fast. Slow down some. People not only need to hear what you're saying, they need to process it too.

9. DON'T ever open your talk with an apology such as, "I'm really not a good speaker," or "I really don't know what I'm doing here." We've heard many people open a speech this way in hopes of endearing themselves to an audience. People want you to do well already. Know your subject and speak with energy and enthusiasm. Then there's no need to apologize. Some of the most powerful talks we've heard were not from professional speakers, but from those who had a passionate message.

10. DO focus on your audience and be as genuine as possible. Focusing on the people and their need to hear what you're saying not only benefits you by helping you be less nervous but certainly helps the audience who may be eager to hear what you're sharing.

If you need to say something, be assured there are people who need to hear it. Obviously, if it's an impromptu speech and there is no microphone, use your voice to its fullest potential.

Here are some DOs and DON'Ts if a microphone is not available:

1. DO project to the last row of people or the person furthest away.

2. DO speak from your diaphragm—not your throat.

3. DO use your hands and body to communicate as well.

4. DON'T neglect the sides or back of the room. Walk around the room.

5. DON'T stand behind the podium. There's no point in standing behind a podium—especially if there's no microphone there! You can carry your notes or cards if you have them. Remember, the podium can bring death to a presentation.

6. DON'T hold your breath! (That would really bring death!)

One important note regarding your audience—be sure the person or persons you're presenting to can ultimately make the yes or no decision. Someone who does not have decision-making authority may burst your balloon before it ever gets off the ground! Unless you absolutely have to go to someone else before you deal with the person authorized to say yes, don't waste your time. Do your research. Find out who makes the decisions, and make your appointment with that person. However, if you are sharing an opportunity with a married person, it's probably best to show it to the couple. The excited one may sway the decisionmaker or be the decisionmaker!

Never take no from someone who is not empowered to give a yes in the first place!

Lead by Being Positive

When the product you are selling is you, making personal contacts and then creating new friendships is a necessary marketing tool. You always want to be meeting new people.

Are you conscious of the way you market yourself? When you are meeting with coworkers, prospects, associates, or others, are you marketing your best self? Are you well-groomed, kind, considerate, and interested in supporting and helping others? When you meet someone and discuss your job or business, what do you say?

When talking to others about what you're doing, are you showing your positive qualities and greatest core talents, or are you complaining about something or someone? Are you edifying, that is, being complimentary of or looking for the good in your bosses, leaders, and others? Or are you being negative and sharing inappropriate information, perhaps in an effort to make yourself look better?

If you work in a corporate environment and are paid for performance; if you work in a factory and desire to move to a higher position; if you are a teacher and want to motivate your students to be excited about your subject; if you're an athlete desiring a top spot on the team; or if you're a business owner seeking to build your business, you can learn to lead others in a positive way regardless of any negativity being generated. Be truthful in representing yourself and, of course, be your best self!

We all feel better, look better, and are more appealing when we recreate ourselves. We can then circulate the new us! We're then being better than our best and maybe even better than some of or most of the rest!

Whenever you are in a meeting with coworkers, or prospective associates or clients, you make a conscious effort to be positive. There is a spark of enthusiasm in the room. Everyone senses it's coming from you. Some are with you and some aren't sure—but that's normal.

Are you marketing your best self? Are you being observed as a person who cares about others because you have a strong sense of compassion and interpersonal ethics? Demonstrate your best self by letting go of any judgment, envy, fear, and prejudice, and by showing others you care about them, no matter how they may be behaving. (Those whose behavior is the worst need your concern the most!)

Speak confidently about what you know; offer ideas without fear of ridicule. Remember, even if someone disagrees, ask your boss, leader, or mentor for clarification about anything you don't understand or how you might refine your approach. It doesn't necessarily mean you're incorrect or that what you're offering isn't valuable. They may just have a different opinion, that's all— no big deal.

When someone else starts complaining about others you work for or with, stay out of that conversation! Begin talking about your job or business in a positive way—being honest, but searching for positives and then speaking them aloud. Don't join in when the negative contingent starts bad-mouthing people, the employer, a leader, an associate, the business, or the latest policy; simply avoid that conversation. Then you can't say something you'll later regret.

If the "doom and gloomers" decide that talking about the challenge and judging the person who caused it is more important than the solution, *you* be the one who decides to move things along in a positive direction. Be the leader in the discussion. Confidently say, "Okay, we acknowledge there's a challenge here; so now what? Where do we go from here? How can we create a win-win situation?" If the meeting veers away from the agenda and people start griping, concur that, sure, there's a challenge. At the same time, however, acknowledge that challenges are opportunities in disguise—and lead the group to focus on the solution.

Be aware, however, that there may be those in your group who may become indignant about your daring and nonconformist response, especially if you went along with the negativity before. This can occur in job or business-related environments, social settings, and other places as well.

Raising the bar, being better than your best, requires the courage and fortitude to stand up to those who want to keep you down. As Abraham Lincoln said, "It often requires more courage to dare to do right than to fear to do wrong."

Don't Take *Anything* Personally

When you employ these ideas to lead in a positive way, don't be offended if someone doesn't like you or what you're sharing. There may be something constructive you can learn from their attitude. The least you may learn is what *not* to do to others, which can be very helpful. Also consider that someone's negative attitude or behavior toward you is more about them than about you. We never know exactly what someone has gone through or "where they're coming from," so don't take a difference of opinion personally. If someone rejects you or what you're offering, be friendly to them and don't let that stop you from sharing something else with them or sharing what you have to offer with others. Stay above it all and keep moving.

Some ideas you have may *not* be that great, and just because you have an idea, doesn't mean you need to act on it. Dan and I constantly throw ideas at each other (I call Dan "the Idea Man")— sometimes they're great, sometimes good, sometimes not so good. That's okay. Sometimes the "season" may not be right for a particular idea. Sometimes an idea may just be the catalyst for another, perhaps even better, idea. What seemed like a mediocre idea last year may be brilliant now—depending on current events, circumstances, or changes in our lives. It's all part of the natural sorting out process. If we were to take everything personally and get upset and hurt when the other one didn't like an idea, we'd never accomplish anything!

As Goethe aptly put it, "Daring ideas are like chessmen moved forward. They may be beaten, but they may start a winning game."

Recreate yourself and then present your new creation of a positive, successful, self-motivated, challenge-overcoming leader to everyone with whom you come in contact. Follow the 90/10 Problem Solution Formula to create a list of the ways you can create the new and improved version of you. Then go out and be better than your best by thinking, doing, walking, and talking like the new you! Walk tall and know that you can sell it only when you tell it!

Always remember what Helen Keller shared: "Be of good cheer. Do not think of today's failures, but of the success that may come tomorrow. You have set yourselves a difficult task, but you will succeed if you persevere; and you will find a joy in overcoming obstacles. Remember, no effort that we make to attain something beautiful is ever lost."

Chapter Nine
Be Unafraid to Fail

"Twenty years from now you will be more
disappointed by the things that you didn't do than by the ones
you did do. So throw off the bowlines. Sail away from the safe harbor.
Catch the trade winds in your sails.
Explore. Dream. Discover."
Mark Twain

A reporter for a local newspaper came to our home office and interviewed us for more than three hours. We were very open with her—sharing our personal stories and backgrounds. She was fascinated by the diversity of our lives, and the number of times we literally had to reinvent ourselves.

The reporter titled her article "Unafraid to Fail." Delighted, we realized the truth in that headline. We've always taken risks, done new things, strived to be better than our best, and believed in ourselves to the point of risking everything to continue our life's work.

We are not implying that we were never afraid or have never doubted ourselves. After all, we *are* human. But, in being true to ourselves—validating our deep feelings and following our heartfelt dreams and goals, and holding on to what we believed to be our best selves at the time—we have been able to remember that *success is realized just beyond the doubt.* This knowledge has gotten us through some really tough times.

In contrast, when we weren't true to ourselves and didn't listen to our deep feelings, we usually failed miserably. But even then, in retrospect, we learned never to compromise our integrity or to doubt what we believe to be right and just. This is a lesson that often repeats itself in our lives.

As Eddie Rickenbacher noted, "Courage is doing what you are afraid to do. There can be no courage unless you're scared."

Being unafraid to fail is the opposite of what most of us have been taught. So, how *can* you live life being unafraid to fail? Our society, which is oriented toward winning, teaches us that being afraid is disgraceful and that failure is shameful. The popular belief is that both should be avoided at all costs.

Being unafraid to fail is the opposite of the average way of thinking in any arena—whether it be in personal, business, or professional life. Some say, "It's too risky. What would we do if we failed?" The stigma attached to failing is so great that it's not unusual for one party to rejoice in a competitor's misfortune, clapping their hands with delight as they watch their rival's stock prices drop, if only for a day.

Why then do we "eat up" stories of people who press on in the midst of seeming failure? Why do we love the underdog? We choke up with tears over movies and stories of people who triumph over unbeatable odds. We love their success because deep inside we believe that *anything* is possible; nothing great is ever achieved without risk and the determination to overcome great hurdles. Deep-down, regardless of what we say, we believe that we are destined to rise above any obstacles put before us.

Our internal desire is to face challenges with courage—to never give up and be victorious. To implement this belief in an often cynical and negative world, we need to trust and believe in ourselves and have the faith that we can do it.

Go for It!

As someone once said, "The positive thinker sees the invisible, feels the intangible, and achieves the impossible."

Famous Shakespearean actor Sir John Gielgud was known for his stellar performances in countless films including *Chariots of Fire* and *Gandhi*. Stage-struck at an early age, he contemplated becoming a set designer, but soon shifted his allegiance to performing. Initially his passion was decidedly one-sided. At one rehearsal, Gielgud's first drama teacher burst out laughing, saying the actor "walked like a cat with rickets." Regardless of that and, in spite of the naysayers, Gielgud pressed on. Not long after his debut, he was at the top of his profession.

You, too, can achieve superstar status—in spite of what others may say.

It took Thomas Edison's getting more than 1,000 unexpected results to invent the light bulb. He never considered these results failures. Instead, he believed each experience brought him closer to success. He learned what *not* to do!

Your success may be only one more step away. So it's essential for you to keep on going. You may be only moments away from finding what works so you can make your dream come true.

Benjamin Franklin is considered to be a great American thinker, a pillar of the United States national heritage. Born the son of a candlemaker with a limited education, few people in his era could foresee that Franklin would become a statesman, inventor, philanthropist, publisher, and revolutionary—and designer of the Declaration of Independence.

You, too, can change the course of history and raise the bar for the rest of the world.

At age 12, movie producer Steven Spielberg got his first 8mm camera. He had made 15 movies by the time he was 18! Unfortunately, though, his grades weren't good enough to get him into a film school. So he began educating himself during a tour of Universal Studios, where it is said that he slipped away to explore the back lots. After finding an empty office, he bluffed the security guards all summer long, returning regularly to the studios sporting a suit and tie. He viewed productions in progress and made valuable contacts. When he was 28, his blockbuster movie *Jaws* grossed $130 million at its first U.S. release. The rest is history.

In another story, devastated by the death of an older brother during World War II, this famous television/radio personality initially withdrew from life. But soon after he started listening to the radio to ease his grieving, he began dreaming of having his own radio show. These events led the now world-famous Dick Clark, beyond any fears of failure, to host the television dance show, *American Bandstand.*

You, too, can astonish everyone with the abilities and talents you possess.

Like these famous people and others, you need to be willing to step out of your comfort zone and take risks to be successful. Don't be afraid to fail. Don't let setbacks deter you. Dismiss the naysayers and keep your eyes on the bigger picture—your vision for your life. Keep in mind the wise words of Theodore Roosevelt: "No man is worth his salt who is not ready at all times to risk his body, to risk his well-being, to risk his life, in a great cause."

People who are functioning at their best do not focus or dwell on "mind trash" or let it enter into their reality.

What Is Mind Trash?

Mind trash is the kind of pollution that destroys dreams, goals, and desires. Mind trash is procrastination, fear, anger, revenge, failure-thinking, envy, jealousy, and hate. It keeps us from success, prosperity, and happiness. In our Western culture, these negative attitudes are not only considered acceptable, but are justified as reality, or worse yet, common sense. As Albert Einstein professed, "Common sense is the collection of prejudices acquired by the age of 18."

We can certainly find many ways to hold ourselves back with our fears, prejudices, and judgments. By doing this, we give ourselves an excuse for never taking a step outside our comfort zone (which is generally not comfortable—just familiar!). It's easy to rationalize with ready-made reasons for lowering our own bar. Here are some of the things we've heard:

> "It's documented that restaurants have the greatest rate of failure," a friend told us. "Common sense would tell me to not even try the restaurant business." Common *nonsense* can keep us from doing something new.
>
> "I've made procrastination into an art form," a college student boasted after waiting until the 11th hour to study for her exam. Consciously created stress and drama often set us up for failure.
>
> Some people fiercely defend their anger and need for revenge because it makes them feel superior. "I'll never forget what they

did to me. They're going to pay for messing with me." Righteous indignation holds us back.

Jealousy and envy can be rationalized as honor. "Look at those rich people. They're probably doing something illegal or immoral to get all that money. I might be poor, but at least I make an honest living." Rationalization to justify our "just-making-a-living" attitude rather than "creating a life," keeps us from moving forward.

Guilt, which is very prevalent, is a form of punishment that people actually inflict upon themselves, often unjustifiably. "I don't deserve to be happy; look at all the bad things I've done in my life." Self-inflicted chastisement is our worst enemy and can keep us stuck.

Narrow-minded people adhere to old beliefs to defend current situations. "How could I advance any further? There's a glass ceiling." Or they may say, "The foreigners and minorities are taking all the jobs." Sometimes they complain, "It's the government's fault. When the other party gets in office, things will be better for me." Or they might comment, "Those leaders are just lucky—they never had it as tough as I do." Erroneous belief systems prevent us from advancing.

So far we've addressed some essential things you need to incorporate into your daily thoughts, words, and actions to become better than your best. Now is the time to address what needs to be *eliminated* from our lives so we can raise the bar and discover who we really are and what we're capable of.

Stop All Negativity by Taking Out the Mind Trash

We often ask our audiences, "How many of you consider yourselves to be positive people?" Most people raise their hands. But just saying we're positive is not enough—we need to honestly eliminate negativity. Negativity leads to cynicism and sarcasm. It steals dreams and brings us down into impossibility thinking. We need to dig in and rout out all the old mind trash that's anchoring us to our circumstances and keeping us from being better than our best.

Here are some things to ask yourself. Even though you are positive, do you ever:

- Engage in negative thoughts or dialogue about yourself or others?
- Use put-downs, zingers, or sarcasm?
- Describe your job or business, family, or current circumstances in negative terms?
- Judge people or situations before you know all the facts?

The following are all examples of negativity that actually lower the bar:

I'm just kidding—Rude remarks are sometimes considered commonplace and funny if followed by "I'm just kidding." It's as if the phrase makes the sarcasm less stinging. Notice the "cute," controlling, negative remarks thrown around by others and you'll start understanding how injurious they can be.

"Half day, Bob?" a coworker quips to his office mate who's finally returning to his desk after being in meetings all morning. How can that possibly help? How does that raise the bar? How will that help increase productivity?

Instead of being appalled by cruel jokes on television sitcoms, we may chuckle, encouraged by a laugh track. Some talk shows revel in audience members spewing downright nasty comments and judgments at guests—the meaner, the better. With adults acting this way, resulting in cynical, angry people ready to defend themselves against upcoming put-downs, is it any surprise that some of our young people are despondent and pessimistic? Is it any wonder that the average worker is unhappy, depressed, and disinterested in work?

Many people are not at ease or at peace with themselves and others. At the worst extreme, this was reflected in the cruel terrorist acts of September 11, 2001 in the United States. We hear of angry employees and kids arming themselves with weapons, then killing coworkers, classmates and teachers. We even hear of furious parents physically abusing coaches and other parents at Little League games! How sad. But remember, what you hear of violence is just a speck of reality. There are plenty of good people doing good things every day that don't make the news.

This is a sampling of how negativity, the foundation of mind trash or brain clutter, pollutes our thoughts. Picture our minds as big bowls filling up with everything we experience. If that bowl is filled with negativity we won't have room for positive, life-affirming thoughts.

Negativity is the single biggest destroyer of happiness and productivity, both at work and personally. We were not meant to think and act negatively. It is *not* natural. We are taught to be negative. We are taught to use negativity to hurt others so we can supposedly feel better about ourselves. We are taught to put down others and ourselves, in subtle and not-so-subtle ways. Consider some of the ways we intentionally or unintentionally lower our own bars:

- Well-meaning parents told us not to get a "big head" when we were complimented or, worse yet, when we said we were good at something. So we learned to advertise our shortcomings instead of our strengths.
- When we expressed happiness, we were encouraged to think something was wrong by being asked questions like: "What are *you* so happy about? Did you do something wrong?" So we learned to look for the worst in situations, often hiding our happiness and feeling guilty.
- When we wanted something new, we were encouraged to feel ungrateful or unappreciative by being asked: "What's the matter with this coat? You should be happy you have something to keep you warm." So we learned to stop asking and stop reaching.
- In first grade, we handed in our ten-question test that had nine answers right. The one wrong answer was highlighted and circled in red ink. So we began to focus on what we were doing wrong instead of what we were doing right.
- When we received a new bike as a gift, our parents apologized for not getting "the best one." So we learned to compare. Now adults, we cannot enjoy a restaurant, a pair of shoes, or even a vacation without making comparisons to others.
- When we expressed what we wanted to be when we grew up— usually something fun and joyful—we may have been told: "That's not going to make you any money. You'll need to get a real job." So we might have learned that work should not be fun, and we may have stopped seeking purpose and instead

sought only money. We might have learned that the opposite of play was work.

- When we excelled at something and doing it made us happy, we may have been told, "Don't be a showoff." This could have taught us to hide the very thing that created passion in our lives.
- As children and adolescents, most of us felt alive and excited about life. We might have been told to "tone down." So we may be careful now not to show too much emotion.
- As children, many of us watched the fire and passion wither from our parents as Mom slowly gave up her dreams and Dad made excuses for not achieving his goals. Sometimes they even blamed us kids. So we might have learned to feel guilty and negative about our own existence. We may have learned not to ask for too much because they said, "you'll just be disappointed." We learned to settle for less, and most of us got just what we settled for, didn't we?

We are not born into this world in defeat; we were born to win. We are destined for success. We are meant to stand tall—not to crawl. We are meant to live—not merely exist. Our minds are meant to soar—not grovel. Could the same God who made the sun, the stars, the sky, the mountains, and the rivers design us to be any less magnificent?

Is it possible that the same God who enabled the animals, insects, and plants to exist in all their rapture and delight, would have somehow made us humans less than worthy of that same exuberance?

How long do we give a child to learn how to walk or talk? We usually let them learn on their own, in their own time frame, don't we? We aren't negative with our toddlers when they fall while trying to stand. We encourage and motivate. As adults, have we changed our tune from "Come on, you can do it!" to "That's stupid! Why would you want to do that?"

Apply the motivation concept to your job or your business! "Come on, you can do it!" needs to be the battle cry for each person entering the company front door or associating in business!

We have 60,000 thoughts every day, but the majority are repeated again and again—and they're often negative! If we repeat negative thoughts day in and day out, week after week, month after month, they become our reality.

Stop the negativity. It's you at your worst—not your best! Here's some things to avoid that could otherwise lead to negative thinking:

The mass hypnosis—The news media, as well as advertising, can condition us to be negative and feel inferior. Observe the onslaught of the negative news and buying suggestions we receive on a daily basis.

Our radio alarm clock wakes us up in the morning telling us about the most negative news. The television weatherperson not only tells us the temperature, but has also come up with a way to make it sound and feel worse by creating a "wind chill" and "heat index." Now it feels like it's 50 below zero or 120 degrees above!

The traffic helicopter reporter reports, "It's a lousy Monday. Traffic is horrible."

A commercial warns you that your spouse won't love you because your breath is bad, and you'd better not ask for a raise because you didn't use the right deodorant. You're told that you have a headache (or will get one soon) when either the kids wake up or hayfever season comes. You'd better take medicine for the indigestion you're sure to get after lunch. And you need to gear up for cold season. By the time you leave home, you have put some product into your body to either plug it up or make something come out. Talk about negative programming!

Playing with our minds, one commercial makes a restaurant's gigantic meals sound exciting and appealing; the next tells us we're too fat and for a small sum a week we can lose the weight we gained at the restaurant. We're convinced to buy things we may not need and informed that we won't have to start paying for them for six months. Yet, in the next instant, we're chastised for our excesses and told we need to consolidate to get out of debt. We're told we can't be happy unless we "look like this, wear these clothes, smell like this, drive this car, eat this food, use this toothpaste, walk this way, talk this way, bank at this bank, invest with this company, buy this anniversary diamond and, finally, we have to die the right way with the right burial plot and the proper life insurance!

With all these ideas playing with our minds, it's no wonder many of us feel negative and unhappy about ourselves.

If you think, even for a moment, that this constant programming is harmless, think again. How often has one negative thought about yourself spilled over to someone else? Just one seemingly innocent, negative thought can start a stampede of negativity—you end up making a negative, condemning remark about someone's appearance, their behavior, or the way they drive. Not only do you affect those around you, but you have just added another sour thought to your own outlook.

Years ago we made a major decision that changed our lives: We stopped watching the news! Can you believe it? We decided we don't need to hear another pretty face telling us over and over again about how bad things are. We decided not to become part of the negativity mindset by repeatedly watching the dramatic presentations newscasters make of all the unfortunate incidents, often created by people who are looking for excitement in all the wrong ways—who are emulating the violence seen on television and in other media.

We are firm believers that all the news we need to know about will find its way to us. People will inevitably say to us, "Did you hear about…?" "Do you know about…?" or "Did you see the story about…?" If we hadn't already heard about the event, someone will most assuredly be more than glad to tell us what *they* heard. We always end up informed—without seeing the incident 57 times on the news!

Being inspired to positive action is occasionally a benefit of watching the news. However, with the constant flow of negative news attacking us, our senses tend to be overwhelmed. Positive inspiration doesn't occur often in the news—surely not often enough to merit the time and energy of watching it.

Compassion is important, but watching and listening to other people's pain over and over again is not. Some people watch the news continually, raising their blood pressures with outrage or spending useless time judging either the victims or the offenders.

Turning off the news may not be easy—until you make it a habit. Sometimes the news is very engaging. It entices you. Many people, however, are addicted to the negativity of the news. In a lot of cases, people have chosen pretty mundane lives. The news seems to add a little variety to their lives or they see someone in a worse situation and rationalize their lot in life by saying something like: "I don't have it so bad after all." It becomes just another success-stealing habit. Remember, do anything for 21 days in a row and it becomes a habit. So why not do something positive? Make a difference in someone's life. Be a great example.

In the morning, people turn on the television "just for the noise." Then, on the way to work, the negative news is repeated on the car radio. At work, people talk about the horrible news with their coworkers and fear builds. They worry about their children when they are in school and when they're walking home from school. In fact, they worry all the time.

Arriving home in the evening, their first intent is to gain information about the day—to feel connected. On goes the local 5:00 news. "Good evening. Here's the local death and destruction." At 5:30, they hear, "Greetings from Any City. Here's the national death and destruction." And at anytime they can tune into a cable TV channel for "World Death and Destruction" every 30 minutes. Worse yet, the news is on during dinner and, finally, before going to bed. If so, your last thoughts and images before bed are fear and negativity. The next morning, unfortunately, the whole routine starts all over again.

You might want to stop doing that—it's just not you at your best! How can you possibly harvest positive thoughts—the thoughts necessary to be unafraid to fail—if your mind is constantly filled with negative images and voices? Remember the Creative Circle? Negative thoughts lead to negative words and actions, helping to create negative experiences and a negative life.

We do not want to indict you or have you feel guilty if you do watch the news. Sure, there are some positive current events stories but, let's face it, the majority of stories broadcast are depressing. They fill us with fear, anxiety, or outrage and lack of hope rather than hope for a better life.

This book is about you being better than your best. It is our objective to help you to live a happier, more productive life. Ideally, don't watch the news at all. Instead, make your own news—build your own success! Be a part of the solution—the positive news in your area and country. Invest the time you used to watch the news and other negative media in a continuing education program of positive books, tapes, and seminars available through your company of organization. We can't emphasize this too much—grow yourself so you can grow your business or profession, and life a happier life.

After presenting one of our "Happy Hour" workshops, a teacher approached us and said, "Last year when you were here, you told us to turn off the news. I took your advice—did my life change! I am so much more positive now. I used to judge my students and my job based on the information I received from the media. I realized this was hurting my students and me. It had affected me in a way I couldn't have anticipated.

"When you suggested turning off the news, I initially thought, 'No way! I'm a history teacher. How could I not watch world events?' But when I stopped watching the news, I didn't have repeated visual images desensitizing me from violence. Thank you so much! I'm much more productive and positive now."

Here's a great positive declaration: "I give up negative thoughts and judgments about others and myself."

No matter how positive you are, you can still be exposed to negative thoughts. Just don't allow them to control your life. Rather, mentally push them away by focusing on your strengths. If a negative thought comes into your mind, don't fight it—say, "Next," or "No thank you." By saying these words, your negative thoughts will leave your mind. This works! Remember, a negative thought cannot exist in the same space as a positive one. It's simply impossible!

Entitlement comments—We may often make negative comments about others based on the notion that they personally owe us something. For example, you're late for an appointment. An old woman slowly wanders across the intersection while you wait impatiently, wasting valuable seconds. The woman doesn't know about your rush. She also doesn't owe you a sprint across the street so you can be on time.

You may think the company owes you because you believe this: "I've spent the best years of my life working for them." But that's simply not true. You spent those years working there for yourself and probably your family. It was your choice—no one forced you to work there. You did it for your own reasons, as we all do. Your biggest mistake may simply be that you think you're working for someone else!

As Mark Twain pointed out, "Don't go around saying the world owes you a living; the world owes you nothing, it was here first."

If you think other people owe you something, you're allowing them to control your emotions if they don't respond the way you think they should. *You* be the master of your emotions. When confronted with a they-owe-me situation, consciously say, "They owe me nothing." Think of the freedom and happiness you will experience by not expending energy in being angry with someone and expecting him or her to respond to your wishes. It's great!

Banish Failure Mentality

Very early in our speaking career, we landed an interview on Chicago's WGN radio with a gentleman named Paul Brian. He was interested in our motivational safety programs offered to children, parents, and teachers in the Chicago schools. The three of us hit it off, and we were invited to return.

After our second interview, Paul gave us some life-changing advice. Danny was expressing impatience about how long it was taking us to become a success. After all, three years had gone by and we were still struggling.

Paul asked if we were willing to take risks. We talked about the many new and different things we had done and how many times we had failed. Back then we measured things in terms of success and failure.

Finally Paul interrupted us and said, "Listen, you guys love what you're doing. People dream about making a living doing what they love. You haven't failed—you just haven't lived enough yet!"

As Winston Churchill observed, "Success consists of going from failure to failure without loss of enthusiasm."

Repeat this positive declaration: "Failure is just an event, but I am a person!"

Every project has a beginning, a middle, and an end—from thought to action to outcome. Your efforts always produce a certain outcome—more focused and longer lasting positive efforts produce greater outcomes. It's really quite simple—until emotions and fears get involved. Our desire to please everyone else can muddle our vision. Also, our need to have things go only *our* way can enter into the picture. If things don't happen the way we envisioned they would, we may feel like failures. We search for an ending that meets our expectations. If the outcome is different than we expected, we may be crushed. We may be so emotionally attached to the particular outcome we pictured that if things don't happen exactly as planned, we're disappointed. As a result, we might constantly be setting ourselves up for pain, anguish, and heartache. Does that sound familiar?

All you seek can be yours. Dream big dreams and thoughtfully set your goals. Focus and place your intention in the helping hands of your own dedicated attention and action. Hold firm to your desire, then do what you know you need to do to make it happen. Go forward with unshakable faith—helping others achieve *their* dreams and goals. In the process you can achieve yours.

The final result of your efforts—the outcome—is nothing more than an event in time. Failure is just an event and success is just an event, as is anything in between these two definitions you've developed. There are millions of events happening to everyone everywhere, all at the same time! Everything that happens is just an event within the journey, which, regardless of the outcome, is the success. No event has power except for the power *you* give it.

Isn't it sad to see someone wallowing down in the dumps after a loss? It is just as sad to see someone trying to use a past success to prove who they are or were—rather than using the present to make a new contribution. Raise your own bar. Live in the here and now.

If an event is not what you desire, do not attach a lifetime of shame and sadness to it. It is what you think, say, and do *after* this event occurs that is *most* important. Choose to go after your goal again or choose to do something else. Choose to let go of any negative feelings you may have and move on to something else that's even *more* exciting! Set your bar a notch or two higher. Give yourself a greater challenge—stretch. But, whatever you do, make a conscious, thoughtful, forward-focused choice!

As George Burns shared, "I'd rather be a failure at something I enjoy than be a success at something I hate."

Nothing fails in nature—The cat crouches low, stalking the robin a few feet from its nose. The feline leaps into the air, claws extended, mouth open and ready. At the last instant, the robin takes flight.

Does the cat immediately turn to see if the other cats were watching? Does he pound his little kitty paw onto the sidewalk, screaming little kitty obscenities? Do the other cats in the neighborhood laugh and tell each other how Fluffy has lost his touch?

Nature shows us example after example of how to take things in stride. Don't view an outcome you were not expecting as a defeat. Keep your overall vision firmly in view. Be flexible about the process and the exact outcome you desire. Focus on your main dream or vision. Don't concern yourself with the stumbles—the obstacles you need to hurdle over or go around along the way.

Think positive thoughts, speak positive words, take positive actions. Believe in yourself and doggedly keep doing whatever it takes. As you do, watch your dreams and goals unfold. Things will happen simply as a part of the process, and you will be amazed at the results! Dr. Robert H. Schuller says it this way:

"*FAILURE doesn't mean you are a failure...*
It does mean you haven't succeeded yet.
FAILURE doesn't mean you have
accomplished nothing...
It does mean you have learned something.
FAILURE doesn't mean you have been a fool...
It does mean you had a lot of faith.
FAILURE doesn't mean you've been disgraced...
It does mean you were willing to try.
FAILURE doesn't mean you don't have it...
It does mean you have to do something in a different way.
FAILURE doesn't mean you are inferior...
It does mean you are not perfect.

FAILURE doesn't mean you've wasted your life...
It does mean you have a reason to start afresh.

FAILURE doesn't mean you should give up...
It does mean you must try harder.

FAILURE doesn't mean you'll never make it...
It does mean it will take a little longer.

FAILURE doesn't mean God has abandoned you...
...it does mean God has a better idea!"

Give Up Guilt

What is guilt? Why do some of us let it affect our lives and deprive us of personal, professional, and business success?

Webster defines guilt as "the fact of having committed a breach of conduct especially in violating the law and involving a penalty." Webster is referring to guilt by a wrongful act. But we are referring to guilt created by ourselves or others that is unjustly perpetrated.

Look at how many times people dish out guilt without even realizing it. We may allow ourselves to be manipulated because guilt is such a powerful negative force. Become the witness. Stand back and observe how guilt is passed back and forth.

We found that by not trying to make others feel guilty if they didn't do something *our* way (which they often don't!), we gave other people the freedom to make their own mistakes so they could learn and grow. This really lightened our relationships.

We started to study the effect of guilt on our personal lives and in our various relationships, ranging from family and friends to strangers. We began to see how people used guilt to manipulate others. But when we do not allow others to succeed in their efforts to make us feel guilty, we move about much more freely and easily.

Don't allow past mistakes to turn into guilt. Perceive them instead as learning experiences. Look at it the way Henry Ford did when he said, "Even a mistake may turn out to be the one thing necessary to a worthwhile achievement." Don't feel guilty about your successes. Don't feel guilty if you have more than the next person. They can have what you have when they do what's necessary to get to that level of achievement. If you choose to get involved in a cause, do it out of a desire to help—a desire to make a difference—not out of guilt.

We choose who we are and what we're becoming. If you do not like who you are or what you're becoming, go back and reread the information on recreating yourself. Then, recreate yourself again, being better than you were in the past. But do not spend another moment feeling guilty about the old version of you—that's over and done with. Move toward your bright future by raising your bar!

Repeat this positive declaration: "I let go of any guilt feelings and move toward my goals and dreams."

How often have you felt guilty about something good that happened to you because someone else made a negative comment about it? Be prepared to fend off others' negative remarks. Sometimes, when you've just enjoyed a deserved success—a promotion, a raise, a new level in your business, a new car—someone will say "...must be nice"—as if you just lucked into your success, rather than worked for it! Immediately you may feel a leak in your bubble of happiness. You can become vulnerable to absorbing their negativity. Don't let that happen. That's not you at your best!

The next time someone who is jealous endeavors to make you feel guilty by saying "Must be nice..." look them in the eye, smile, and say, "It *is* nice!" Don't for a moment let their envious comment diminish the enjoyment of your achievements, successes, or happiness. It *will* be very nice to have the success and happiness of accomplishing your dreams and goals.

"Please release me. Let me go"—Remember that old song? Releasing your guilt does not mean you won't ever feel badly about past mistakes. That's normal and natural. But as Mark Twain said "...you will be more disappointed by the things that you didn't do than by the ones you did do." You have the choice of being bitter or allowing yourself to grow and be better than your best. Use past events to strengthen you now—either as valuable lessons learned or as memories of victories to remind you that you can do what's essential to make any dream or goal a reality. Learn from the past. Choose to be better this time than you were before. Raise your bar!

Guilt makes us pay for the same mistake over and over again. Forgive yourself, let it go, and move on to better things.

- Forgive yourself for any petty and jealous thoughts you may have had. That was then; this is now.
- Forgive yourself for any pain you may have caused others, knowingly or unknowingly. If you would have known better, you would have done better. Now you know.
- Forgive yourself for any mistakes you may have made. Get up, get over it, and get going again.
- Forgive yourself for any mean and hurtful things you may have said to people you love. Apologize. Ask for forgiveness. It's up to them whether they choose to forgive you or not. Either way, be okay with it. Then move on with your life.
- Forgive yourself if you have been cheap and stingy with anyone. Become a giver. Be kind and generous to yourself and others. No one can steal from a giver and you'll feel great about yourself.
- Forgive yourself for any time you've wasted. It's over. Snap out of any self pity you might have. Start right where you are to invest your time wisely working toward your goals and dreams.
- Forgive yourself for any unfair judgments you may have made. From today on, judge nothing and no one—you can never have enough information to judge anyone. Besides, it's not our job as people to judge each other!
- Forgive yourself for any past racism or prejudice you may have exhibited. Imagine how you'd feel if you were the recipient. Be accepting, kind, and inclusive from now on.
- Forgive yourself for any inappropriate behavior. Adopt a loving attitude and a new approach.
- Forgive yourself for not being your best when you knew you could have done better.

Today is a new day. Recreate yourself. Show the world the fine person you really are! Never feel guilty for doing your best to better yourself or for endeavoring to develop yourself to go to a new level in your business or profession. Don't let others who choose not to move on hold you back or make you feel guilty about making progress! Guilt is corrosive. It is like acid on metal. Don't give it and don't take it!

Release Anger and Revenge, and Start Forgiving

Anger and revenge are the ego's way of saying "You can't do that to me." Anger is nothing more than an attempt to try to make someone else feel guilty about what they've done that we didn't like. Look at the times in your life when you were extremely angry. Think of the source of that anger.

Here are five questions to ask yourself:

- Do you allow personal problems to affect your work or business performance?
- Do you often find yourself thinking angry thoughts about others?
- Do you ever think about getting revenge on those who have hurt you?
- Do you find yourself thinking angry thoughts about past events?
- Do you hate anybody?

Have you ever tried to convince a coworker or associate that he parked too close to your line? Did you think the action was wrong because, "The least he could do is respect me, my car, and my space"?

Have you ever been angry at your college-aged son for not choosing the career or business *you* wanted for him? Was your attitude, "How could he do that to me after all I've done for him"?

Have you ever been angry with an associate or coworker because she moved ahead of you by reaching a new level in her business or getting a promotion at work? Was your perspective, "I've worked my business just as hard as she worked hers. Why did she make it instead of me?" Or maybe it was, "She couldn't possibly be better suited for the job than I am—look at the long hours I work."

Have you ever been angry because the person driving in front of you was poking along? Did you call them some choice names under your breath?

Do we mistakenly think that the whole world revolves around us?

Perhaps someone parked too close to your coworker's or associate's line when he pulled in, and he had no choice but to park closer to your line.

Maybe your son would be miserable doing what you want him to do. Just because you are a teacher, for example, is it fair to expect him to be one too—even if he'd rather own a business? Isn't it reasonable that he decide what he does with *his* life? Remember how you may have tried to please your father and worked in a job you hated?

In your business, maybe you weren't as persistent. Or, at work, it's possible that not only your work performance was evaluated in determining the promotion, but your negative attitude of "entitlement" was evaluated as well. Maybe your coworker had a more positive, service-oriented attitude. Perhaps you were never being considered for that promotion. Did you remember to ask for it? Or did you just assume you "should" get it?

Maybe the person ahead of you was driving the speed limit, but because you left fifteen minutes late for work or an appointment with a prospect, you were frustrated with yourself.

Remember, as Albert Einstein said, "Anger dwells only in the bosom of fools."

This month, release just one person from your anger and strive to see the situation from his or her perspective. Release him or her, and release yourself too—your anger hurts *you* most of all. Choose not to be angry with the person sitting across from you at work, or the neighbor whose leaves blow over onto your sidewalk. Let go of your anger. Learn to take a deep breath and adopt a peaceful, caring state of mind. Set yourself free. You will be free from the tense, stress-filled feeling you have every time you see or think of the other person. You will live longer and be happier, and be able to accomplish much more. You will think more clearly.

Anger is an emotion like any other. However, pent-up anger can lead to domestic abuse, road rage, workplace violence, divorce, health problems, and addictions. To manage anger effectively, you first need to define the cause of your anger. Anger is usually a secondary emotion masking a feeling you believe isn't safe to express—like embarrassment, hurt, shame, jealousy, fear, or frustration. If we feel vulnerable because of the emotion we're feeling, we may mask our vulnerability with anger. By identifying our true feelings and sharing them with someone who unconditionally loves and supports us, we are less apt to react in a way that's harmful to others or ourselves.

As we talked about earlier, we may also get angry if we think someone isn't doing what they "should" be doing for us. It's called the "you-owe-me" attitude. No one really owes us anything—everything we do is for our own reasons. Thinking that people "owe us" just sets us up for letdown after letdown.

Write down this statement and always remember it: "No one owes me anything!" When you adopt this belief, you will reduce 95 percent of your stress!

Find ways to positively channel the energy the anger brings. For instance, as children, Danny and I both had acts of violence committed against us. We were angry with those who hurt us. Danny suppressed his anger and I acted out on mine, hurting myself and everyone around me.

Years after the actual incidents we decided to release the hold the anger had over us. How? We took our negative energy and turned it around, pursuing positive activities. We worked out and honed our martial arts skills. We took classes in police science, crisis counseling, and rape prevention. We taught more and more classes on women's self-defense and child safety. We spoke on college campuses nationwide about overcoming trauma and preventing violence.

This was all part of our process of letting go. Within that process we developed not only careers, but also our life's work. What a blessing that turned out to be! We began by examining our anger—where it stemmed from—and deciding that we didn't want to be angry anymore. We no longer wanted revenge.

Forgiveness is in direct conflict with the ego. Revenge and the need for revenge is based on the ego's idea of self-importance. The little lift derived from revenge is usually overshadowed by the response of the intended victim of your revenge. First you seek and get revenge. Then the villain you set up to receive that revenge begins to avenge your act of revenge. The cycle continues. You get what you give.

This is not you at your best. This is not coming from the most developed part of your mind. So, stop it right now! Learn to let any anger go by forgiving. Why wait? Start now. Compassion is more powerful than anger. Forgiveness is greater than vengeance.

Now let's explore the three keys to forgiveness:

Identify the Hurt—*The First Key to Forgiveness*

Be clear where the hurt developed and who delivered it. Search your mind for the details about when and how it happened, and especially how you contributed to it! Then, rethink the hurt. As Marcus Aurelius said, "Take away the belief 'I have been harmed' and the hurt will disappear. Take away the sense of hurt and the harm itself is gone." Know that some of the greatest contributors to our betterment as people come from the most unloving people with the most unskillful behavior. We can grow tremendously in overcoming our challenges with these people. After all, they show us how *not* to be or do.

Let Go of the Problem—*The Second Key to Forgiveness*

Choose to do whatever it takes to get past the problem. Empty your mind of mean thoughts about the other person. Empty your mind of everything you could have done differently. If you would have known better and were in a more loving state of mind, you would have done better. If the same were true for them, they would also have done better. If it is your desire to change, then allow the other person to recreate him or herself too. Give them a chance. But, at the same time, don't necessarily expect them to do so. The best way to initiate change in your relationship is to treat them more compassionately.

Healing the Hurt—*The Third Key to Forgiveness*

Forgiveness is the path to healing. Help others in your life get past their problems. This will help you to reinforce doing the same for yourself. Create ways to release your anger toward people who hurt you. For example, write a letter to yourself as if it is from one of those people, explaining his or her behavior as much as you can from that perspective. Then toss it. Find peace in forgiveness. It is a gift you can give to yourself.

Say throughout the day whenever necessary: "I let go of my anger and the need for revenge for they serve no one, especially me."

Here are some other ways you can reduce stress (and eventually anger) in your life:

- Rather than leaping right out of bed at the last minute and hurrying to begin your day, get up 15 minutes earlier. Take time to plan and pray. Starting this way provides an uplifting foundation for the rest of your day.
- Live in the present moment. Anxiety increases if we brood about a past event or fret about something in the future.
- Approach an event that you would normally react to stressfully with a can-do, positive attitude and it will boost your energy.
- You are allowed mistakes. Be easier on yourself—learn to look for the blessings and move on. For example, what did you learn from your mistake?
- Give yourself some credit. Take a moment each day to give yourself a pat on the back for all the good things you do. Appreciate the great balancing act that enables you to manage multiple responsibilities at home, at work or in your business, at your place of worship, in your children's school, in your community, and elsewhere.
- Invest time each day to create peaceful, serenity-inducing images in your mind. During your work or business day, occasionally pause and imagine yourself in a tranquil setting—alone on a beach listening to the waves, enjoying hearing and seeing birds chirp and splash in a birdbath, or perhaps stretching out on the grass looking at the sky—whatever soothes you.
- Change your eating environment. Get out of your workplace or business and enjoy a meal in the park. Occasionally eat by yourself in silence. Eat slowly, enjoy your food, and be thankful for it.
- Observe your breathing. When we are relaxed, our breathing is slow and even. However, if we are anxious or upset, we tend to breathe irregularly.
- Take a brisk walk. Exercise burns off excess adrenaline that fuels feelings of anxiety and stress. Listen to a positive, uplifting inspirational or motivational tape as you walk.

- Practice hospitality. Greet people with a big smile. This will help you and others to feel good and, in turn, it will give you a deep sense of ease, calm, and peace.
- Just say no. You don't have to accept every project, every invitation, and every request anyone has. Focus your attention on your dreams and goals.
- Relive a happy memory. In a time of stress, look back and remember a pleasant experience or satisfying moment in your life. Smile and relish the memory.
- Everything doesn't have to be *perfect*. It's amazing how much stress can be eliminated when we decide that we don't need to have a perfectly clean house, a perfectly manicured lawn, and perfectly behaved children. Perfectionist expectations are not only unrealistic but unnecessary. Learn to let go and relax with the inherent imperfections in life.
- Walk in someone else's shoes. You'll feel a lot better. Do your best to see a conflict or difference of opinion from another person's point of view. As bestselling author Stephen Covey says, "Seek first to understand, then to be understood." When people realize you're doing your best to understand their perspective, they are relieved and feel the compassion you're emanating.
- Don't bring work problems home or home problems to work. When you pull into the driveway, take a minute to orient yourself as a transition before entering your home, being with your family, and perhaps to building your home-based business, if you're fortunate enough to have one.

Stop Procrastinating—*Just Go Do It!*

Procrastination is fear, and fear is negative faith. Procrastination originates in insecurity and a lack of self-confidence. What is it that is holding you back? Is it success that you fear? As Joan Baez said, "Action is the antidote to despair."

If you were to get that job or promotion, or achieve that new level of success in your business, are you afraid you won't know how to handle it?

Are you concerned about what everyone will say? Are you afraid they won't accept you?

If you continually procrastinate, you continually postpone reaching your dreams and goals. Flush out the fear on a moment-by-moment basis. Talk with your leader, mentor, or boss to achieve the success you so earnestly desire. Find out, step by step, what you need to do.

Fear leads to procrastination—which leads to even more fear. If you worry about what others will think, you're likely to stop yourself from performing at your best. Fear of failure leads to procrastination and stops you from being productive in the present moment.

Are you afraid that you do not have enough knowledge on the subject or enough experience? Heed this advice: Do first and learn as you go!

The Procrastinator's Promise

" I'll do it all tomorrow, for tomorrow never
comes. I promise you for sure I'll do it then.
I shall positively feel a tremendous lot of zeal.
I'll be a whirl of dynamism once again.
I'll do it all tomorrow, that I promise faithfully;
I'll rise all bright and eager in the dawn!
I'll astonish all the neighbors with my energetic
labors, and I'll be the go-est getter ever born.
I'll do it all tomorrow when I've planned the
thing with care. I'll buckle down and get to it,
come what may! What I really can't allow is to do
it here and now. For I've planned a lot of nothing
for today."

—Author Unknown

How about those goals you are always talking about? What have you done *today* to put you closer to achieving them? What did you do yesterday?

Ask yourself, "What's holding me back?" Take the time to write down a list of things blocking your way. Use the 90/10 Formula to examine your fears and overcome them. Use the 90/10 Formula to determine your next steps. By doing these exercises, you have started on your road to success.

Stop procrastinating now! Get started! Why wait? Start Now! Mother Teresa heeds us, "Yesterday is gone. Tomorrow has not yet come. We have only today. Let us begin.*"*

Remember the phone call you've been putting off for weeks— maybe months? Make that call today. What about those monthly continuing education seminars you've been meaning to plug into? Buy tickets now! Weren't you talking about getting out of debt and becoming financially free? Haven't you been dreaming about building your profession or moving to the next level in your business? Haven't you wanted to take more of a leadership role at work or in your business for quite some time now? What do you fear?

Franklin Roosevelt said, "The only thing we have to fear is fear itself." Fear is a state of mind. And you can take control over what's going on in your mind. Don't let fear keep you from living your life to its fullest.

And Frederick Wilcox noted, "Progress always involves risk; you can't steal second base and keep your foot on first base."

Be better than your best by becoming an agent for positive change. Teach others that there is no such thing as failure. Help them succeed. In helping others, you always help yourself. Remember that by working together, all things are possible. Avoid giving or receiving guilt and manipulation. Channel the energy of anger into tremendous productivity. Eliminate negative thoughts and words from your daily "diet." Start saying, *"I am a positive person."*

Why wait! Start now! Now is the time! You are the person! As Winston Churchill observed, "To every person there comes in their lifetime that special moment when they are figuratively tapped on the shoulder and offered that chance to do a very special unique job to them and fitted to their talents. What a tragedy if that moment finds him unprepared or unqualified for that work."

Chapter Ten
Play to WIN—
With Inspiration Now

"To be nobody but yourself—
in a world which is doing its best,
night and day, to make you like everybody else—
means to fight the hardest battle which
any human being can fight, and
never stop fighting."
E. E. Cummings

When we play a game, of course we want to win. That's our goal. Hopefully, we also aim to enjoy the process as much as possible! Whether the game we're playing is starting or building a business, moving up in the company, making a sale or bringing on a new associate, running a department or running your household, we want to succeed. We feel great as we move forward and reach our goals, one after the other. This helps to keep us motivated.

By "playing to win" we're not referring to the traditional win-lose paradigm. From an enlightened perspective there is no such thing as a loser. Even if the outcome—for example, the score—shows that someone had more points, it doesn't mean that the one with the lower score didn't have an opportunity to "win." They might have successfully done their best and learned what they need to do next time in order to do better. Every coach knows that in a so-called loss the team learns more about themselves than they do in a victory. So, who is truly the victor?

This is not a call to abolish competition. We have participated in many diverse competitions and have always delighted in a friendly challenge. As Napolean Hill noted, "Success in its highest and noblest form calls for peace of mind and enjoyment and happiness, which comes only to the man who has found the work he likes best."

We'd like to present to you what may be a brave, new idea to you regarding work or doing business. Begin to think of your work and business experiences as *play*. Wrap your mind around the concept of work as a fun game, and think of going out to play that game each day. Then take it even further—*play the game to win!*

What if you used the same approaches in your life that you would use if you were training for an athletic or academic event? You would enter the competition with the express intention of winning—*losing would not be an option*. True winners are victorious even after a loss, using the loss to help them learn, grow, and become better prepared for their next competition.

Danny competed for the American Karate Association's (AKA) National Lightweight Kickboxing title. Before each match he would cross the ring to his competitor's corner and ask him to personally give him his best. He would say, "Don't hold anything back." This was not out of cockiness or macho bravado, but out of a pure desire to compete at the highest level. Dan never wanted to enter a fight thinking "This guy is no good," or "This is going to be easy." How could that possibly inspire him to compete at *his* best?

When Danny won the AKA title, he had the personal satisfaction of knowing that he truly deserved the win—he had played the fairest game with a motivated competitor. Over the years, there were, of course, matches that Dan didn't win, but what he gained was immeasurable. Even if he lost, he knew his opponent had given his best. This inspired Danny to be better than his best.

Playing to WIN absolutely does not mean in any way destroying or humiliating others. We can compete with others without hating or even disliking them at all. Have you ever witnessed a true winner before, during, and after an event—excited, poised, graceful, confident, respectful, persistent, and humble?

WIN—*With Inspiration Now!*

Playing to WIN is operating your life from a place of inspiration, not desperation.

From desperation, you feel helpless and alone.

With inspiration, you have no problem asking others for help and support. Consider this:

> " *From desperation, you fear change.*
> *With inspiration, you are open to learning*
> *anything new . . . even if it scares you.*
>
> *From desperation, you are always looking for*
> *that one big chance to turn the tide.*
>
> *With inspiration, you know that steady*
> *achievements add up to huge successes.*
>
> *From desperation, you fear someone*
> *else may outshine you.*
>
> *With inspiration, you respect and admire this*
> *person's diverse talents and learn from them.*
>
> *From desperation, you feel drained at*
> *the end of the day or evening.*
>
> *With inspiration, you may be tired, but you feel*
> *exhilarated—knowing you're doing*
> *what it takes to make it happen!"*
>
> —Danny and Marie Lena

If you were to *always* come from an attitude of pure *inspiration*—not effort or desperation—how would your life change?

Let's step out of the box. Imagine yourself playing to win. You are the champion in your arena. You are the winner. You are the prime example of victory. Imagine yourself having the experiences winners have. You have a great winner deep within you waiting for your permission to come out and play!

To be better than your best, play to WIN!

- When playing to WIN, your thoughts are focused and direct.
- When playing to WIN, your daily habits are intended to enrich you in all ways.

- When playing to WIN, you realize the importance of rest and relaxation periods…"time outs." If you're out late doing your job or business, you squeeze in a 30-minute power nap the next day.
- When playing to WIN, you depend on and trust other team members or business associates.
- When playing to WIN, you know the importance of faith.
- When playing to WIN, you are inspired and motivated by the accomplishments of others.
- When playing to WIN, you recognize that the joy is in the game itself, not just the outcome. There is truth in the phrase, "It's not if you win or lose, it's how you play the game."
- When playing to WIN, you courageously step forward and let your talents and skills shine.
- When playing to WIN, you're inspired to be better than your best.
- When playing to WIN, you know who you really are, where you are, what's next for you, and what you need to do.

Playing to WIN can truly create a new foundation of motivation! "With Inspiration Now" can be your new motto. WIN in your personal life! WIN in your professional or business life!

Living life this way every day will bring dramatic changes. You will feel alive and have the confidence of a winner. Everyone will notice the difference. You will release the real you who has been waiting to appear and play to WIN.

Begin thinking with a winner's approach as you face life's daily challenges. Think, "How would the greatest winner ever known handle this situation or respond to these troubles, tragedies, and trials? What would such a winner do? How would the world's greatest winner handle my current situation?"

Then, think, say, and do what your heart, mind, and body guide you to do. Trust yourself. Show the world your true greatness, your purpose, and that you have a laser-like focus on your goal!

Play to WIN—With Inspiration Now!

Play BIG

Aaron was starting first grade. As friends of his parents, we were delighted to be invited to the bus stop on his first day of school. He was wearing shorts and suspenders, a collared shirt, new socks, new shoes, a baseball cap turned sideways, and he was carrying his action-figure lunch box. He was *so* excited!

Of course we made a big fuss. He asked, "Dan and Marie, today's my first day of first grade. Do you have any advice for me?"

"Of course we have advice for you, Aaron. Listen up."

Aaron's eyes widened in anticipation.

"Take a lot of risks; ask a lot of questions; raise your hand when the teacher says 'Who can answer that?'; volunteer for everything; introduce yourself to everyone; ask if you can go first when no one else wants to; make friends with everybody; respect everyone; play nice; trust yourself; be nice to the girls; share what you have with everyone; sing powerfully; give others a chance to speak; help clean up; stand up for yourself; be the first to get there and the last to leave; sit in the front row; learn something new each day; and always remember to—play BIG, shine, and walk tall!"

Imagine the delight of having a youngster standing in front of you asking, "Do you have any advice for me today?" They're really asking, "How can I be better? How can I raise my bar?" How you answer them is of utmost importance. Wouldn't you give them the best advice you could? Wouldn't you take a moment to explain how they could be better than their best? Of course you would!

Suppose a person with great faith was to wake up in the morning before their work or business day and ask God, "Do you have any advice for me today?"

Can you imagine God responding, "For today, why don't you just try to blend in?" Not in a million years! As E. E. Cummings advised, "It takes courage to grow up and turn out to be who you really are."

The message of blending in is taught in many ways. Parents literally hold their children back from sitting in the front row at their places of worship and at other functions, fearful that they might stand out. In school assemblies, when students begin to raise their hands to answer questions, friends may give them the "look," and their hands may drop. Some teachers, supposedly hired to share knowledge, actually discourage their students from answering questions by belittling them when they do! Blending in is a mediocre mentality that denies you the opportunity to contribute fully in all areas of your own life!

In what way would blending in ever benefit anyone? With all of your wonderful talents and skills, why would you want to hide them from the world?

You have so much to offer others by speaking up, letting yourself shine…by showing up and being your best self.

What a powerful example you can set by…

- Being brave enough to answer a question—even if you might be wrong.
- Sitting in the front row at your place of worship, unafraid to show your faith, ready to receive the message from the minister, rabbi, or priest.
- Speaking only positive words about yourself.
- Volunteering to give a speech or presentation at work, in your business, or at a community function.
- Walking to the front row at a seminar or meeting, unafraid of being noticed, ready to listen and take notes.

Anyone who ever told you *not* to do these things was mistaken. Anyone who belittled you, causing you to put your hand down, was just expressing their own fear. Anyone who ever humiliated you in front of the class for an incorrect answer was doing you an injustice. Anyone who suggested to you that you should blend in and not be noticed was intentionally or unintentionally holding you back from stepping up to the plate. It's that kind of average thinking that leads to the "I'm a nobody" mindset. This way of thinking will only make you feel powerless and that you don't make a difference.

As Jawaharlal Nehru, the first Prime Minister of independent India, shared, "The policy of being too cautious is the greatest risk of all."

So, get out of your comfort zone and play BIG! Life begins at the edge of your comfort zone. Let the world know what you're all about. By playing BIG, you will have increased vitality. You won't worry about making mistakes. You'll understand that anyone who does anything worthwhile makes mistakes. You will take more risks. You will meet and befriend more people. Your example will draw others out of their shyness. You will bring smiles and joy to others. You will spread happiness, love, joy, and compassion because you are in a state of true expression of who you really are. This attitude is contagious! Others will be inspired to shine too!

Someone once said, "Dance like no one is watching, sing like no one is listening, work like you don't need the money, love like you've never been hurt, and live like it's heaven on earth."

These words have been said before in different ways in countless books, songs, and sonnets over the centuries. Many people, from religious leaders to business leaders to nations' leaders to poets, musicians, and artists, have endeavored to tell us to face our fears of greatness and unleash our potential. Isn't it time for you to make this concept functional in your life? Why wait? Start now!

Go ahead and shine!

Recall often the encouraging words of Guillaume Appolinaire: "'Come to the edge,' he said. They said, 'We're afraid.' 'Come to the edge,' he said. They came, he pushed them…and they flew."

"**L**earn to serve. Let go of your ego and offer assistance to others."

—Danny and Marie Lena

Chapter 11
Success with Soul

"Let me win!
But if I cannot win, let me be brave in the attempt."
Motto of the Special Olympics, Inc.

When we speak of winning and success, we need to address ethics. Some people seem to succeed in life and business or personal relationships by forgoing ethics. The outcomes of their efforts are really not wins. Eventually, a high negative price will be paid—usually the loss of friends and family, and deterioration of personal health—both physically and mentally. Sooner or later ethical people will learn the game of the unethical person and they won't want anything to do with him or her anymore.

When it's almost over and your life is nearing its end, don't you want to know deep inside that you've treated others fairly and ethically? As you succeed in life, don't you want it to feel right? Don't you want to feel honorable and good about your accomplishments—to be able to speak about them without shame or embarrassment but rather with a sense of integrity?

Sometimes If You Lose, You Still Win!

If company A lost an account, prospective associates, or a contract to company B due to company B's corrupt practices, illegal doings, or improprieties, then it is not really a loss for company A. Company A gains a great opportunity to discover who they are. The controlling parties in company A can demonstrate what they will or *will not* do to land an account. They can exhibit character, values, and ethics. So, even in the loss, there is a win—a bigger win than achieving something dishonestly and always being afraid of losing it, being found out, or both.

In defining who they are *not*, company A can show who they truly are. Company A can honestly present itself as a group of people with reliable, ethical business practices, thereby attracting clients and associates they feel good about serving and working with. They can feel good about the product, service, or opportunity they provide.

Can that really be considered a loss? Did company B really win? Maybe there is a short-term win; but for the most part, company B will always be looking over its shoulder, worried that a company C will come along and do the same thing to them that they did to company A!

Interpersonal Ethics

Interpersonal ethics is key to resolving the previous situation. It's having kindness and compassion and reflecting those qualities in our behavior, as well as seeing the same in others—sometimes admittedly well-hidden, but nonetheless there and able to be nurtured and brought out. This is how we can learn to treat ourselves and others in more mutually beneficial ways. We can better accept and embrace our differences and work more peaceably toward a common end. When we learn to perceive each other as warm, special, loving fellow human beings—like we are all part of a close-knit family—we'll be on our way toward more interpersonal ethics and a happier, healthier world as a whole.

Talk about raising the bar! As Danny and I sorted all this out, we have become *much* more aware of the way we treat others. We decided to pursue a new goal—to build interpersonal ethics more solidly into our operating system and make it part of our foundation, putting it into action immediately. We set out to develop understanding and respect for every individual of every race, physical capability, gender, age, religious conviction, and other differences. This does not mean we necessarily agree with everyone's belief systems, but we respect their right to their own way of thinking.

We made *the choice* to become this way—it was different than the way we operated for a great part of our lives. We decided to change—to reinvent ourselves—to raise the bar. When we started accepting and not judging others, we found we had much more energy. We felt better and spent less time worrying about how "wrong" everyone else was. As a result, we were happier too.

We learned that in spite of obvious human differences, we all have a lot in common. We discovered that our lives were not just about us—we all affect each other to one degree or another. We're all part of the human family. We began telling others about the benefits of inclusion. Begin now and...

- Start thinking differently about your coworkers, team members, and business associates. Look at each person as an amazing human being. Some are amazingly wonderful; some are amazingly challenging! Either way, people are diverse, unique, individualized, and essential to all productivity and success. That's why you have a job or are in business—to produce, to make money, and to hopefully enjoy the process.
- Become an agent of positive change. You be the leader of such change. Begin immediately to speak uplifting, motivating, empowering, positive, supportive words to yourself and others. This is important in terms of helping people change their negative attitudes and move on to achieve certain goals. Create a positive team, recognizing that every team, division, group, and organization has a special and unique personality. "Pump up" your team's personality by noticing, appreciating, and acknowledging their positive traits. You alone can start the wheels turning to create a new corporate or organizational soul. Start getting people on your bandwagon. Find allies. Form a supportive group and the change will happen more quickly and easily.
- Snap into action! Why wait? Start now! Take actions that unify—actions that include everyone. Make a clear decision to build the team, to lift the members, to raise your own bar, and to raise the company or organizational bar with the concept of T.E.A.M.—*Together Everyone Achieves More*. Your actions will demonstrate how important this is. Show everyone the value of having a good time at work or in your business. Let's make the time you're working at your job or in your business, every single day, something special.

Success with S.E.L.L.

Success with S.E.L.L. began as a motivational sales tool we used when presenting workshops on ethical business practices. Ethics can sometimes be a hard sell. Companies want profit and, sadly, money is often the priority instead of the people. But if we presented the bottom line benefit of ethics, we knew we would get their attention.

We hung a poster on the wall and spelled the word "S E L L" vertically down the left side of the poster in six-inch letters. Participants were instructed to write SELL along the left border of their notepads. This formula helps people sell or share any product, service, opportunity, or idea to prospective clients or associates. This gets their attention! Here goes…

- *Sacrifice your ego.* In other words, as we shared before, it's not about you. It's about serving your clients' and associates' needs. It's about listening to what your prospect, client, or associate is endeavoring to convey to you. Stay focused on the client or prospect, not on making a sale or an association. Know your product, service, opportunity, or idea but don't boast. Arrogance can destroy a potential sale or association and turn off prospects and clients forever. No one likes an egomaniac. Put your ego aside and humbly come to the table with the attitude of "How can I serve you?"
- *Empower the prospect or client.* Give him or her ways to say yes. Allow the prospect or client to tell you about their wants, needs, dreams, and goals. Honestly share with them how they need your product, service, idea, or opportunity to achieve them. Show them how they can afford it, can't live without it, and can have it today. Use any ethical (and, of course, legal) methods or tools at your disposal. Never try to intimidate or manipulate the client or prospect to pressure them into a yes. Always be relaxed, friendly, and considerate of their needs and wants. Not only is it the right thing to do, but it bodes well for future communication. They are more likely to welcome your calls and visits rather than avoiding you! Set it up so they feel good after purchasing what you are selling or associating with you in business—so they feel excited about signing on the dotted line, definitely not pressured or stressed.

- *Live with enthusiasm in the experience.* Revel in the experience of helping someone change his or her mind. Love the idea of the resistant prospect or client because, in their resistance, they'll tell you their qualms. You'll learn more about the people you're serving and their wants, needs, goals, and dreams. Experience patience as you assist a client or prospect from being a cautious individual with arms folded, looking at his or her watch, to a person who is smiling and excited! You want to end up doing more than just making a sale or association—you want to create a positive win-win relationship that endures for years with an advocate who sells you, your product, service, idea, or opportunity to others.
- *Love your product, service, idea, or opportunity.* Feel great about what you are offering. How convincing can you be if you're selling Chevrolets but driving a Cadillac! Be loyal to what you are doing. Use your own products and services, implement your idea, and take full advantage of your opportunity. Love the idea that what you are sharing serves a meaningful purpose. Believe that it is the best on the market. If it's not the best, maybe it has *other* features like cost effectiveness, improved delivery time, or the chance to leverage with the association of other like-minded people. Be congruent and honest—say and do what you mean and mean what you do and say. Do what you believe in and believe in what you're doing. If you don't believe in what you're sharing, maybe you need to learn more about it or move on to sharing something else.

The response from our audiences, whose initial reactions to the ethical approach were often at first reluctant, always ended up being one of overwhelming joy and relief. Salespeople were happy that they could actually be ethical. We gave them permission to be kind in business—amazing! *Let go of your ego. Empower the buyer or prospective associate. Live in the experience. Love your product, service, idea, or opportunity.*

To our delight, we began receiving e-mails, letters, and phone calls from participants long after we had presented our seminars.

"I have to tell you, that formula not only worked for me in sales, but I applied it to my personal life! Wow! Things have really changed!"

One lady told us, "My husband and I were having problems in our marriage. I used your formula—and it worked! I was always blaming him for our lack of communication. Once I put aside my ego and made it safe for him to speak truthfully, he became empowered to tell me things I really needed to hear. Our relationship has changed dramatically! The environment in our house is now one of openness and freedom to speak the truth. We even use this with our children. Our family is much closer now. Thank you!"

After receiving this kind of feedback, we became even more excited. Here was something that could really help people change their lives—not just sell products, services, ideas, and opportunities. When people use this in *all* areas of their lives, it could be monumental in changing the climate of communications.

Applying the SELL Formula in Your Personal Life

We revised the formula somewhat to make it appropriate for personal lives and relationships. Use this formula in any situation. It will provide clarity and understanding, helping you observe the situation from someone else's perspective. You'll see yourself changing—judging less and loving more. If that's not being better than your best, we don't know what is!

1. Sacrifice your ego but remember who you are. You are here to serve others as an equally valuable person, however, you are no one's slave, and you don't deserve to be mistreated.
2. Empower everyone. Lift others up, help them excel, and help them realize how special and unique they are.
3. Live with enthusiasm in the experience. Fully experience the experience with all of your senses.
4. Love unconditionally. Love without parameters and without conditions. Love people even if you don't like them, their behavior is disagreeable, or you don't choose to associate with them outside of your job or business activities. Remember, the people who need your love the most are the ones who are behaving in the most unlovable ways.

Let Go of Your Ego and Serve Others

Learn to serve. Let go of your ego and offer assistance to others. (Some say ego is an acronym for Edge God Out!)

No matter what "position" you're in, no one is beneath or above you in intrinsic value. Our greatest nonviolent, peacemaking leaders humbled themselves to others. Martin Luther King, Gandhi, Mother Teresa, and Jesus all gave generously of their service to people.

Be generous while respecting yourself and others as follows:

- As a parent, you are there to guide and help your children, but you are not their slave.
- In your marriage, you are there to serve each other, but you are not a doormat to be used and abused.
- At work, you are there to do the job asked of you, but not at the risk of your integrity.
- As a student, you are there to learn, but never stop questioning the belief systems taught to you.
- As a subordinate, you are there to take orders, but not harassment, provocation, or inappropriate demands.
- As a businessowner, you are there to serve your prospects, clients, and associates, but not to be taken advantage of.
- As a citizen, you accept the role your political leaders play, but not with blind faith. You still have a mind and heart of your own which you express as needed.

Let go of your ego, but remember who you are as follows:

- Stand up for what you believe in.
- Speak truthfully, clearly, and without reservation.
- Find your voice and let it be heard, even if you're afraid of being rejected.
- Welcome compliments gracefully, with appreciation.
- Humbly accept accolades for your achievements.
- Express your desires.
- Embrace and utilize the wisdom you've gained from living.
- Trust and follow your heart, balanced with your keen mind.

Empower Everyone to Excel

"Keep away from people who try to belittle your ambitions. Small people always do that, but the really great make you feel that you, too, can become great," Mark Twain so insightfully noted.

To empower is to enable or authorize. By empowering everyone you meet to excel, you provide a comfortable, accepting, supportive atmosphere, letting others be who they truly want to be without restrictions, conditions, or limits—unless they're encroaching on your rights. You remind people of their uniqueness by giving them the means to express it. Have the attitude of "I am special and you are special too."

When you honor others, you give them respect. By recognizing and pointing out someone else's strengths, you enable them to consistently and better express themselves. Empowering everyone you meet to excel allows them to see their own specialness. In lifting another person up, you automatically raise yourself up. Go forth and empower everyone you meet to excel as follows:

- Give others a platform from which to shine.
- Say yes to other people's dreams. Be encouraging, and understand that no one is given a dream without the ability to accomplish it.
- Offer positive suggestions so they can reach their goals and realize their dreams.
- Help others win and succeed.
- Be there to listen when needed.
- Express enthusiasm for other people's ideas.
- Buy inspirational materials and use and share them.
- Be the source of ideas and support for others.
- Be genuinely concerned about other people. Express that concern openly and confidently.

Preston's Challenge—A fantastic cook, Dan was making veggie fajitas one night when he realized we were out of tortillas. The meal was almost done, so I said I would quickly run to the grocery store, promising to be back within minutes.

At the supermarket, as I was searching for the tortillas, I noticed Preston in the Mexican food aisle. Preston is a young man who works as a stock boy and bagger. Though he is what most people would call "mentally challenged," I call Preston "an innocent." He is pure, sweet, childlike, and a "gentle giant."

That night Preston was very focused on labeling cans and being in a hurry, I quickly asked, "Preston, where are the tortillas?"

He looked up in a distracted manner and pointed above my head. "They're right over there."

I reached up, grabbed the package, and turned to thank him when I saw that he had his head down, looking sad—very unusual for his normally upbeat self.

Realizing that Preston needed my concern, I faced him directly, hoping he'd raise his face. "Preston, how are you? Is something wrong?"

He looked up at me, took a deep breath, shrugged his shoulders, and sighed, "My life has no meaning."

Shocked, I put my tortillas down, grabbed him by the shoulders and looked into his eyes. "Why would you say such a thing?"

"Someone told me that no one would ever want me...that I don't know what real life is like and I'll never find anyone to love me," he shared dejectedly.

I immediately felt anger for the person who would say such a mean thing to Preston, thinking it was probably one of his co-workers jealous of his positive attitude. But in that moment, I realized that this was not about me and my feelings. This was about Preston!

"Preston," I said, "You are a wonderful person. You're kind. You're handsome. You always have a positive attitude. You make people smile and always have something kind and nice to say.

"You take care of yourself. You're neat and clean. *Anyone* would be lucky to know you and to love you. It was very unkind for that person to say that to you. And their opinion of you needs to be none of your business."

Preston looked surprised.

"Don't you ever allow anyone to tell you what you can't do. If someone tries, it only means *they* think they can't do it! Preston, you stay just the way you are. You are not only likeable, you are lovable. You are capable of changing the world! I know my world would be different without you. I would miss you if you weren't here anymore. And do you know what, Preston? The person who said that to you just doesn't know any better. Forgive them. If they would know better, they would do better.

"Now, hold your head high and don't let them get to you, okay? You are special, you are unique, and I love you."

"You do? Why?" he said with wide eyes.

I repeated my reasons. They were the same reasons. Maybe he just needed to hear them again!

Preston then hugged me hard right there in the aisle by the jalapeño peppers! He squeezed me for about a minute, thanked me, and returned to labeling cans.

I felt so good, tears welled up in my eyes as I smiled and said goodbye. I got halfway down the aisle and he yelled to me, "Hey, lady, lady!"

I wiped my eyes before turning to look at him.

"You forgot your tortilla shells!"

It wasn't about the tortilla shells. It wasn't about my being in a hurry. It *was* about taking the time to empower another person to excel at being *who* he is. As I related the story to Danny, he felt my happiness. We shared the good feeling together, and then he warmed up the veggies.

They were the best fajitas I ever had!

Live With Enthusiasm in the Experience

Remember yesterday, dream about tomorrow, but live today!

Living enthusiastically in the experience begins with enjoying the present. How can we be more in the moment every moment of our lives?

First, begin by letting go of the past. Get out of yesterday. People either live in the sadness or the glory days of the past. Consider friends and loved ones. Think how often they speak of events from the past—"the good old days of college, the high school championship we won, my first love in high school. Do you remember back when we went camping with the Scouts? Remember when we all got our driver's licenses? Remember the vacations we took as kids?"

We're not saying you shouldn't reminisce about happy times. Fond memories are pleasing to the heart. However, don't dwell in the past. Living today based on yesterday is a futile attempt to recreate the past. It will bring you unhappiness. You're not the same person you were then. You've changed. The world has changed.

You may recall everything from back then as being perfect. However, memories are sometimes unreliable. And trying to live in a perfect moment from the past robs you of a perfect moment in the present!

Instead of living with enthusiasm in the experience, some people live in the memories of yesterday or the vision of tomorrow. They never have time for today. Unhappiness and frustration result from constantly taking one step forward and two steps back. Relationships are destroyed when one or both parties focus only on the past or look only to the future for happiness—foregoing the joy of today.

We need to tell you that this book is written by two of the world's biggest dreamers! We continually plan for the future. Our past, by and large, has been wonderful and exciting. And, although we lovingly reminisce about it, we recognize that the past is just a memory. We don't try to recapture the past or allow ourselves to be stuck there.

When we discuss our vision for the future, we recognize that we will create it using our own free wills. We don't expect everything will go exactly according to our plans. We know that having such expectations could lead to feelings of failure and non-accomplishment. We would then miss the beauty of the world unfolding before us as we pursue what's on our minds and hearts.

A sign on our computer says: *Be open to whatever happens.*

Look back on the happy times of yesteryear, and enjoy the present thoughts, but keep your primary focus on today. We need you right here, right now. Your children need you right here, right now. Your spouse needs you right here, right now. The world needs you right here, right now. You can only contribute in the present.

How can you possibly be better than your best if you're focused on the past?

The Then/When Trap

Another time trap that keeps us from living in the present is our constant anticipation of the future.

"I'll be happy when: my ship comes in; I lose a few pounds; I win the lottery; when the kids get out of school; the rain stops; I get the raise."

Be careful of this trap. Then and when are interchangeable. They can keep you just circling around, now and forever.

This circular trap called "I'll be happy when or then" is dangerous. It can suck the life out of you.

- "Back then when I was thin" could easily become "When I lose a few pounds…"
- "Back when the kids lived at home" could easily become "When they return for the holidays…"
- "When I finish my book" could easily become "Then I'll be somebody special."
- "When I get the right job" could easily become "Then I'll get respect."

Like a hamster running on a spinning wheel, the when/then trap can have you constantly spinning, going nowhere. Where does it leave you? Often you are exhausted at the end of the day, having made no forward progress. The next day, again, you will get on the spinning wheel, trying to get to that elusive place of "then I'll be happy."

In continually looking to the future you lose the experience you're having right now. When you lose this moment, literally nothing has been accomplished. Nothing is new. When someone asks you "How are you? What's new?" you can honestly answer, "Nothing." And you'll be absolutely right.

Children are good examples of living in the now. They can teach us such great lessons.

Andrew's Focus

A few years ago we moved into a new home. As Dan was moving boxes, a little neighbor boy approached, saying, "Hi. My name is Andrew. Do you wanna play?" He was about four years old, and had red hair, blue eyes, and freckles.

"Sure," Danny said, and he continued carrying boxes into the house.

On Dan's next trip out, Andrew repeated, "Do you wanna play?"

Dan said, "Sure…that would be fun."

"Okay. Let's play now," said Andrew.

"You mean you want to play *now*?"

Confused, Andrew asked, "When did you think I wanted to play?"

Over the weeks and months that followed, Andrew taught us much about present moment awareness and the importance of now.

One afternoon he rang the doorbell and asked Dan, "Do you wanna ride bikes?"

He was standing next to his bright red Big Wheel™ (tricycle) with flames on the side. Dan looked over his shoulder at me. He had been on the computer for five hours already, and his neck muscles were getting tight.

I said, "Go ahead. Have fun."

Dan went to the garage and dusted off his mountain bike. Using our sloped driveway as a ramp, Andrew and Dan propelled themselves twice around the cul de sac.

Then Dan explained, "Andrew, I'm going to have to go back to work in a little while."

Living as he always did in the present moment, Andrew said "Okay," and drove off without looking back!

Months later, on Valentine's Day, the doorbell rang. No one was at the door, but hanging from the doorknob was a construction paper heart filled with candy. Written in Mom's handwriting was "Happy Valentine's Day! Love..." Then Andrew wrote his own "A" in crayon. When I called later to thank him, Andrew answered the phone.

"Thank you so much, Andrew. That was really nice of you."

Andrew repeated what he often hears us say to him. "You're welcome. You are special."

We spoke for a minute or so, and I began to run out of things to say to a four year old. I asked the typical adult question, "So, Andrew, what are you doing now?"

He paused a moment, processing my question.

Then he replied, "I'm talking on the phone. What are you doing now?"

Present moment awareness is not being in the past, and not being in the future. It is focusing on and living in the now. To progress to living with enthusiasm in the experience," you need to involve all your senses—sight, sound, touch, taste, and feeling. Pay attention to what's happening by incorporating your body, mind, and heart in the experience.

To live enthusiastically in the experience, combine focused attention with sensory perception and integrate both into your thoughts, words, and actions. The intensity of your life experience will be filled to the max because no experience will be casual. Everything you do will have meaning. Every encounter will be magnified. You will no longer operate on "auto-pilot." Everything becomes an adventure. You will have a conscious connection to your moment-to-moment happenings, realizing that nothing will ever be routine again.

Live with enthusiasm in the experience today, and your tomorrows will take care of themselves!

Love Unconditionally

Take inventory. Who can you begin to love unconditionally, without requirements, starting today: your spouse, your coworkers, your leaders, your business associates, your family, your children, yourself?

This is the most challenging part of the formula.

It's easy to love the sister who comes to your home on holidays, bringing food she's prepared. Her children behave and they help clean up. It's easy to love the son who has great grades and stays out of trouble. It's easy to love the supportive parent who's always there for you. It's easy to love the friendly, helpful coworker or associate. It's easy to love the conscientious student who sits in the front row, waiting to answer questions and help you pass out papers or clean the whiteboard. It's easy to love a friend who shows up to help you move. It's easy to love your twin who gently slides down the stairs in stocking feet on your birthday morning, quietly tiptoes to your room, and whispers, "You stay in bed. I'll make breakfast. And as far as any presents go, your love is all I need."

However, it's tough to love a twin who stomps downstairs, kicks open your door, turns on a *bright* light, puts out a hand and commands, "Get up. You owe me some presents."

These examples are all simple and exaggerated, but they seriously demonstrate the parameters we may put on who and how we will love. Yet the measurement of the love we can experience is directly related to how much we can love those we deem unworthy of our love—the obnoxious neighbor, the unruly student, the critical coworker or associate, the unresponsive parent, the angry tollbooth attendant, or the bedraggled beggar on the street. "How can I possibly love this person when I am so unlike them?" we might wonder.

The Beggar in Boulder

One warm, sunny New Year's Day, Dan and I meandered around the picturesque town of Boulder, Colorado, in shirtsleeves like the rest of the tourists. There was an air of celebration as sun-kissed sightseers took a break from the ski slopes to enjoy the high energy of the people in this vibrant town. The streets were pulsating with a diverse mix of people—couples in love, college students on break from classes, tour groups of seniors, wealthy travelers dining in the open air, families buying souvenirs, and amongst all this fanfare was a beggar.

He was a man about 30 years old, sitting on the ground near a newspaper box outside a busy restaurant. Holding a bottle of beer in his bag, he was yelling at passersby to give him money.

"Hey you! Got any change? Gimme some," he demanded with a drunken slur.

Dan and I were about 15 feet away from him, sitting on a cement ledge outside the restaurant, contemplating seeing a movie. We were also watching people's expressions as they passed the beggar. Some begrudgingly threw change at him, careful not to touch him. Others diverted their eyes, so as not to make eye contact, then quickly skirted past. Satiated customers leaving the restaurant sported guilty faces as the beggar yelled at them, "Now your stomach's full, but what about me? Got anything for me?"

Some threw him dollar bills. Still others looked at him with disdain as if to say, "Get a job." They kept their hands in their pockets and made haste past the corner. It was obvious that most everyone was uncomfortable as they passed this boisterous beggar.

We watched for nearly ten minutes, discussing how we could love this man unconditionally. We decided we needed to see ourselves as similar to him. But how were we like him? We never begged on the street asking strangers for money.

Then Dan remembered the quote, "There, save by the grace of God, go I. Here by the grace of God I am." We repeated the phrases out loud several times. But still, we've never begged on the street. So *how* could we be like him?

Then we remembered asking strangers for money when we wanted them to invest in a project. We've asked family and friends for loans. We've looked at wealthy people and *expected* them to give us money just because they had it. We thought people owed us something because we were touting a good cause—our work with children. Soon we began to see ourselves in this man. We sent him prayers of unconditional love. "There, save by the grace of God, go I. Here by the grace of God I am."

Dan wanted to get a newspaper so we could see the starting times of the movie. To buy one, he would need to stand in front of where the beggar was sitting. Earlier, Dan had emptied the car ashtray of loose change to exchange for dollar bills. Now, he stuffed his hand into his pocket, grabbed the change (about $6.00), and told me, "I'm going to give him this. And I'm going to give it to him with total love, not like I owe it to him, not like I pity him, not because I feel guilty." It just felt right to me.

As Dan put his quarter in the newspaper box, the man looked up and said, "Hi, buddy. How ya' doin'? Nice day, huh?"

Dan responded as if he was a casual friend, looking him in the eye, saying, "It's a great day. Happy New Year!"

"You too, buddy. Have a nice day," said the man.

The beggar never even asked Dan for money! He didn't even sound drunk! He was totally sober and coherent. He didn't say one unkind word to Dan. It was amazing! This man felt the unconditional love from us. We saw him as an equal and he responded as one. He had no reason to ask for money!

The power of unconditional love bathed us in happiness. We went to the show and saw *As Good as It Gets.*

Where unconditional love exists, fear has no place. Unconditional love is totally without judgment. It has no past, for the past would imply an attempt to control. It has no future, for that would make it subject to conditions and expectations. Unconditional love is without reservation—absolutely and completely.

Unconditional love is not concerned about whether love will be returned. It is not based on whether the object of the love behaves the way we think they should. Unconditional love is being open-minded about associating with people who are different than you. Unconditional love means you can disagree with someone and dislike their behavior and still love them. Unconditional love is not withheld in an effort not to be hurt. Unconditional love is safety and freedom. It does not separate from others. In fact, unconditional love involves seeing yourself in others and reaching out with empathy.

Reversing the SELL Formula

Each part of this SELL formula is important and presents a great challenge. People unwittingly use it in reverse and go full speed ahead—in the wrong direction!

Instead of sacrificing ego, some people come from an attitude of arrogance, believing no one can teach them anything. They know everything about everything, and they are always right. They are ego-driven. They feel the world revolves around them. Do you know anyone like this? You can see through their facades—which often hide a deep sense of unworthiness. Usually you avoid these people because of their lack of consideration.

Then there are those who, instead of remembering who they are and believing in their inherent worth, completely discount their own feelings and desires in an effort to inappropriately please others. They are masters at letting go of their egos, but they end up feeling dumped on because they almost never get what they really want and need. And to add insult to injury, they often don't do very well at appropriately pleasing others either! As a result, they become resentful, angry, and wallow in self-pity. They feel like no one understands them which, of course, may be largely true. How could anyone understand them when they never express the truth about their feelings? They are often martyrs—looking good on the outside, but furious on the inside.

You will not find happiness for yourself by only satisfying others' needs. You need to satisfy your own needs as well.

Instead of empowering everyone to excel, many people, perhaps unknowingly, disempower others. They put other people down and often make fun of them. In disempowering others, they speak for them, ask their questions, ridicule their dreams, laugh at their ideas, shut them down in conversation or talk over them.

They also openly humiliate others in front of a group willfully and with malice (either physically, intellectually, or emotionally), gossip, or speak falsehoods about them. They complain that "no one can do it as well as I can," yet they never give others a real chance to excel.

Some parents criticize children for being lazy, yet they often do the children's homework and constantly clean up after them. They complain how teenagers are irresponsible, yet "out of love" they fix their mistakes "so they won't get hurt." A family caregiver resents taking care of Mom, yet doesn't give Mom any responsibilities which would empower her to take care of herself.

Assuming any other person cannot exist without you is arrogant. It robs the other person of self-esteem. Doing everything for everybody does not empower them. It disempowers them—not to mention wears you out! Remember the Chinese proverb: "Give a man a fish, you feed him for today. Teach a man to fish, and you feed him for a lifetime."

The Conditional Love Dilemma

Let's look at how someone can get lost and create a dilemma by loving with conditions. Some people love based on whether they'll be loved in return. It's similar to withholding love in a relationship because you're concerned that you'll get hurt. Your conditions become "I'll give you some if you give me some. I'll give you more when you give me more. If you give me less, I'll give you less. If you do this, I'll do that."

What a sad, lonely way to live. Ironically, the qualifying factors you set on others receiving your love will be the same conditions they set for you! That is why, in a world filled with so many lonely people, we still have so many lonely people. Many of us are afraid we might get hurt if we love fully, so we may settle for little or no love at all.

We were once there, and we know about these things. We used to come from ego, disempowerment, living in the past, and conditional love.

In the process of recreating ourselves, we realized that occasionally we were doing things that made us not be our best—not to mention *better* than our best! So we stopped doing them. We replaced the negative thoughts, words, and actions with new, positive ones.

Raise your own bar by sacrificing your ego, empowering everyone to excel, living each experience fully and enthusiastically, and loving unconditionally. Learn to forgive yourself for your past mistakes. Then forgive others—for yourself. Recreate who you really are! As Ralph Waldo Emerson shared, "What lies behind you and what lies in front of you pales in comparison to what lies within you."

"**E**ven if you're not the CEO or a high level leader yet, you can shape the direction of the corporation or organization by being better than your best—by raising the bar on your ethics, integrity, and personal character."

—Danny and Marie Lena

Chapter 12
Creating a
New Heart in Business

"In the time we have, it is surely our duty to do all the good we can to all the people we can in all the ways we can."
William Barclay

Here we refer to heart as being fundamentally kind, generous, well-intentioned, and forgiving. It is the opposite of the way many people in business have been taught. It is having an upward-moving, open-minded, compassionate way of thinking and behaving.

We've challenged you to raise your own bar by using the Creative Circle to change your experiences. By minding your own business—focusing on your own thoughts, words, and actions, you begin this change. When enough individuals take this new attitude into the work world—into businesses and corporations globally— we *can* make this a much better world to live and work in. It starts with each of us, right where we are, no matter how thoughtless any of us may have been in the past.

Martin Luther King observed, "Man must evolve for all human conflict a method which rejects revenge, aggression, and retaliation. The foundation of such a method is love."

The shift is already happening. Innovative thinkers and pioneering leaders are changing the face of the business world, unafraid to challenge the way things have always been done. New ways of thinking regarding inclusion, diversity, leadership, and ethics in business have shifted us to a more compassionate and aware business arena. This has been amplified by the upwelling of kindness generated worldwide in response to the terroristic atrocities in the U.S. on September 11, 2001.

Something that isn't reflected in business statistics is the measure of the caring hearts of its people. There are companies and organizations that reflect the genuine concern and respect shown throughout the levels for their employees and customers, clients, and associates. You don't have to ask—it's beautifully evident in how everyone is treated.

If there are disagreements, which are bound to be a part of the mix, the people involved work things through and strengthen the strained relationships—bringing themselves to an even higher level of caring for each other. In some cases, they are let go because they undermine rather than uphold the fine values and mission of their company or organization. More and more emphasis is on respect, values, listening open-mindedly, having a sense of community, integrity, having fun and being kind, nice, and compassionate. They utilize and appreciate people rather than use them up and throw them away. How heartening!

So, fortunately, the business world is getting more and more in touch with the hearts of the people—the collective heartbeat of the corporation or organization. After all, without its people, no business would be anything!

Leadership with Heart

Quoting the great Emerson again, he said, "What you are speaks so loudly, I can't hear a word you're saying."

Corporate and organizational leaders need to display the very values and behaviors they desire from employees and associates. In other words, the leader needs to walk the talk.

When corporate or organizational leaders merely go through the motions, their messages have no true meaning for employees and associates. For instance, when a company implements diversity training simply in order to avoid lawsuits, employees will sense that the training is a ploy if their leaders fail to treat them with respect.

If the leader demands honesty from employees and associates but compromises his or her own integrity for sake of the bottom line, the message is clearly "Do as I say, not as I do." This creates a lack of respect for the leader which will eventually negatively affect the company's or organization's morale and productivity. Unfortunately, judging by the number of corporate scandals and companies paying settlements for various types of discrimination lawsuits, we obviously have a long way to go before the majority of the business world truly gets warm and fuzzy.

Even if you're not the CEO or a high level leader yet, you can shape the direction of the corporation or organization by being better than your best—by raising the bar on your ethics, integrity, and personal character. Take on a leadership role and accept responsibility. Choose to demonstrate your own style of leadership:

- **L**ove what you are doing.
- **E**xpect the best.
- **A**ttitude—have a positive attitude always.
- **D**elegate authority—encourage people to grow.
- **E**xample—set an excellent example through your actions.
- **R**esponsibility—take ownership for success and failure.
- **S**urround yourself with doers and positive people.
- **H**andle situations calmly. Think! Answers will come.
- **I**ntegrity—others look to you for moral conduct.
- **P**raise others for qualities and efforts, not just accomplishments.

As Peter Drucker says, "Management is doing things right; leadership is doing the right things."

We Need to Stand United and Appreciated

Have unconditional understanding. Respect and understand every individual, including those who are different from you.

Recognize the human family. Know, regardless of our obvious human differences, that we are all in the same human family, interdependent to one degree or another. We are a worldwide family living in various communities.

Open the lines of communication. Create a workforce or group of associates willing to change and participate in new strategies by accepting and honoring others' ideas, perspectives, and innovations. Make it safe for people to share their ideas.

Be more observant. Notice more and be more sensitive to the feelings of others. Value an individual's contributions, in whatever form they come packaged.

Empower the individual and the team. Develop effective strategies for the implementation of each person's core talents within your system. Then allow and encourage each one to be an integrated, equally worthy part of the team.

For businesses to be better than their best, each employee or associate needs to first and foremost realize that they are part of a team. Together, individuals comprise the whole of the corporation or organization. To convey that message, we need to focus on not only just tolerating each other, but on accepting and valuing one another. Paramount to the success of a team is the ability to see and appreciate the uniqueness and specialness in everyone.

The Company You Keep

Reduce negativity and resentment and replace them with positivity and acceptance. This will lead to increased creativity. People will receive greater cooperation from each other through mutual respect. People will feel empowered to move forward in the company or organization and, in turn, help others excel without fear of loss themselves. The new forward-thinking companies and organizations are willing to participate in new strategies by being open to and embracing change.

Twenty-First Century Diversity

Maya Angelou shares, "It is time for parents to teach young people early on that in diversity there is beauty and there is strength. We all should know that diversity makes for a rich tapestry, and we must understand that all the threads of the tapestry are equal in value no matter what their color."

The topic of diversity is so popular now that almost every company has adopted or is adopting a diversity policy. There are hundreds of consulting firms addressing the issue from all sides, ranging from forced etiquette mandates on how to avoid lawsuits to proper protocol in boardrooms abroad. It is amazing that certain people sometimes need to have the idea of respectfully behaving toward others written into law before they'll do it!

We, Danny and Marie, tend to address the issue from a deeper and more layered perspective. We think that you merely need to look at nature to appreciate the kaleidoscope of shapes and colors that co-exist and assist in each other's growth and development.

Diversity is intrinsic to the world's development. Valuing diversity is essential to the growth and survival of business in this 21st century. Diversity is something we all have in common. It would be pretty humdrum if we weren't such a diverse population. Celebrate it and enjoy the variety it adds to your life every day.

Here are six ways to value our diversity and raise the corporate or organizational bar:

1. Learn new ways to appreciate our differences.

   - Find out what is and is not acceptable behavior.
   - Appreciate that each person has a very individualized set of qualities.
   - Search for new solutions for the challenges created by prejudice and hatred.
   - If you have employees, set aside time during at least one workday each quarter for educational diversity programs in a social setting. Create activities designed to uplift and empower each other.

2. Understand differences and form solid, positive relationships.

   - Encourage each employee, coworker, or business associate to contribute their unique qualities to create an organizational power greater than the sum of its individual parts.
   - Implement strategies aimed at forming positive business relationships grounded in honesty, trust, and understanding.

3. Create an atmosphere of acceptance, support and encouragement for our differences.

- Have or attend regularly-scheduled diverse group activities.
- Willingly offer to each other whatever information and knowledge is needed to get the job done or to build your business.
- Know that we have all had different life experiences and realize that those experiences have given each of us a different understanding of "what is so," i.e., we all have different perspectives.

4. Empower everyone to excel by recognizing their strengths and helping them with their weak areas.

- Motivate each other to be more—give short, you-can-do-it pep talks to each other as needed.
- Be an edifier. Tell all who will listen how fantastic your employees, coworkers, associates, and leaders are.
- Be supportive and appreciative, rather than envious, of your coworkers' or business associates' accomplishments. Applaud them enthusiastically.
- Encourage your employees, coworkers, or associates to participate in a continuing education program of books, tapes, other learning materials, and seminars to grow themselves and their professions or businesses.

5. Keep up with and be excited about the developmental changes in your business or industry.

- Be open to new ideas and technologies by using all of the latest proven digital communications technology available to you in your job or business.
- If you're an employer, level the playing field by implementing appropriate and cost-effective upgrades to computer systems on a regular basis. Then retrain your people on the latest hardware and software so they are well equipped and better able to move up in the company.
- Honor the wisdom of age and the enthusiasm of youth.

6. Teach concepts of interpersonal ethics to others by your excellent example.

- Learn new ways to respect each other, and teach these ways by modeling positive behavior.
- Stress loving acceptance in your words and actions. Eliminate judging.

Judgment + Stress + Negativity = Lost Productivity

Judgment is a form of negativity that drives us away from cohesiveness and productivity. We may tend to judge people based on their clothes, financial status, skin color, ethnic background, religious beliefs, tastes and preferences, age, marital status, job, car, house, gender, education or lack of it, what school they attended, whether or not they have children, and so on.

Judging others creates stress in our minds. It makes us focus on the negative. We can never really have enough information to make a judgment.

It's probably happened more than once to you—it certainly has to us. We've made a judgment or developed an opinion about someone based on the limited information we had—only to find out that we were incorrect and unfair because the real story was completely different.

We saw a sign once that read "Today I will judge nothing and no one."

We're challenging you to practice nonjudgment for ten minutes. For just ten minutes, no matter what you see or hear, you will not judge. You will simply see the situation as it is and accept it. Say this positive statement: "I accept this situation exactly as it is." If you find yourself judging a person or a group of people, change the statement to "I accept this person exactly as he or she is," or "I accept these people exactly as they are."

If ten minutes seems too long, set up a daily motivational minute. Practice total acceptance for everything, everyone, and every group you encounter in that minute. Make this practice a habit.

Stop yourself if you are tempted to verbalize a judgment about someone else, hoping that someone will refrain from judging you if you have a challenging day or act in a way that is unusual for you. Once you give up the need to judge, you'll notice that a weight will be lifted from your heart, leaving room for you to be positive and productive. You will begin to better understand and appreciate diversity in others as opposed to comparing them to you and your standards.

Acceptance, understanding, respect, love, compassion, and openness have proven to produce happier, more productive employees, associates, team members, and businesses. Imagine people in your company or organization implementing these attitudes. Picture yourself being more like this.

People need to feel that they are contributing their lives to a greater cause. What could be greater than knowing that we all matter and that we all affect one another? Wouldn't most people pay more attention to how they treat others and do things if they better understood their impact?

They would no longer treat their professions or businesses as just jobs—people would actually enjoy contributing in what they do! No matter what profession or business they're in, individuals would know that they are making a difference. They would realize that no job or business is insignificant, that every person has value and worth and, therefore, something to offer. Everyone wants to feel valued, to make a difference, to leave this world in a little better condition than when they got here. This goes beyond corporate or organizational heart—this is the reason we were all created!

Heart is the emotional, caring part of human nature. This is who you really are. When it is your desire to recreate yourself, to intentionally raise your bar, to become better than your best...when you sincerely desire to change for the better, then do as Gandhi said, "We must be the change we wish to see."

Unless we change individually, we cannot change collectively. For generations many of us have been waiting for other people to change first. A change of heart cannot be legislated. It needs to come out of conviction. Let's all go out and do our part to change the world! Why wait? Start now!

Closing Remarks from Danny and Marie
You Can Go That Way If You Want To— Everything Is a Choice

Years ago, we were invited to keynote a leadership rally sponsored by the Indiana Department of Education. Since we had a rental car, the sponsors asked if we'd mind picking up another professional speaker whose flight was scheduled to arrive just after ours. They said, "You can't miss this guy. He's a Mississippi State Trooper named Pete Collins." Although we had never met Pete, we had certainly heard of him. He's nationally known for his talks to teenagers on alcohol and drunk driving.

Pete wasn't difficult to pick out of the airport crowd. Built like an athlete, he was tall, with wide shoulders and a tiny waist. His uniform was impeccable—wrinkle-free, with sharp creases in his shirt and trousers, topped with a no-nonsense trooper hat worn low on his forehead. The airport crowd parted to let him pass—not out of fear, but to make way for this energetic man. He had a fast, determined gait.

Sometimes you have a familiar feeling about certain people when you first meet them. With others it may take a few minutes, or even a few years. We instantly felt like we had known Pete our whole lives. It started with his handshake which was firm, sincere, warm, and respectful.

Marie asked Pete if she could take his briefcase for him. "No, ma'am, I've got it," he said in a down-home, folksy Southern accent.

I started to open the back door of the car for him and he politely stopped me, saying, "You don't have to be my chauffeur." Then he reached over and opened the door for Marie. Talk about raising the bar! Sincerely, Pete responded to Marie's surprised "Thank you!" with "My pleasure, Ma'am." (From that day on, I've always opened the car door for Marie.)

Pete got into the back seat. He didn't sit on the left side and he didn't sit on the right side. Pete sat dead center in the backseat. He immediately snapped on his seatbelt. As we did the same, I adjusted the rearview mirror and there was Pete, perfectly framed in the backseat with his trooper's hat pulled down low. Have you ever tried to drive with 200 pounds of policeman staring at you in the rearview mirror? I realized that this was going to be a l-o-n-g ride.

But I sat up straight. I positioned my hands correctly at ten and two o'clock on the steering wheel. I changed the rock n' roll radio station to smooth jazz for easy listening. I checked *all* my mirrors before moving into traffic. With every lane change I conscientiously used my turn signals and checked my blind spot. Soon, we were on the expressway going no more than 54 miles per hour. This experience gave new meaning to raising the bar while driving!

Pete's a great guy (and he *did* finally take off his hat). The travel time went by quickly. We exchanged stories about kids, about keeping safe, about giving presentations, about how excited we all were—being the opening and closing presenters at the weekend rally. Soon we were at our hotel.

The Hyatt was ahead of us on the left, just across a small intersection. To pull up to the entrance, all I had to do was make a quick left and a quick right. I clicked on the left turn signal just before the light turned green. When I pulled out to make the turn, Marie's arm swung out to stop me and she yelled, "Dan, don't go that way!" I slammed on the brakes, jerking to a stop. Looking to where she was pointing, I saw a large sign with an enormous arrow pointing right at us. It said: One Way. Do Not Enter.

I paused. Looking down the street to my left, I thought, "It's only 50 feet, even if it is a one-way…one quick left and a quick right, and I'm there. I live in Chicago and I drive the streets every day. I've even driven in Los Angeles and New York City. I can make it. This is Indianapolis—a piece of cake. Besides, it's no big deal." Marie's words rang in my head, "Dan, don't go that way!"

As if reading my mind, Pete's voice echoed from the back seat, "No, Dan. You can go that way if you want, but it's going to cost you 150 bucks. It will cost you $100 for the bond and $50 for the ticket. And if you make that left, we could hit someone head-on. Then, not only are we going to be affected by your decision, but so are the people in the other car. And don't forget the friends and families of passengers in both cars, and all the other people who would be affected by the accident.

"Also, how about those 3,000 teen leaders we're supposed to talk to today? We'd run the chance of not being there. Not only would they not hear our message, but the meeting planners would be stuck without their key speakers."

Needless to say, I was embarrassed and felt like I certainly could have known better. Furthermore, we were talking to the teens about setting an example! Marie and I smiled at each other. We knew that Pete's statement, "You can go that way if you want, but it's going to cost you..." could be applied to many choices we make in life.

I did take the correct way to the hotel entrance. It took more time in the short-run, but we got there without incident. Along the way we realized an invaluable lesson: one little shortcut that seemed harmless and insignificant could cost us a lot in the long-run. It was a metaphor for our life decisions. The consequences of taking the so-called easy way out *always* exacts a price. Are you willing to pay that price?

You can choose to never question what your best is and suffer the consequences of a lifetime of mediocrity and sameness. You can choose to struggle and look at everything as a problem or burden. Then you will have to endure, in addition to the other challenges you'll face, self-imposed hardships and unnecessary sacrifice. You can choose to hold onto the past, paying the price with bitterness, anger, and resentment.

You can choose to lie, cheat, manipulate, and withhold the good you have to give, but you'll suffer the consequences of that behavior—a world that seems to be out to get you. You can be unwilling to take risks, but you will never know the exhilaration of courage in the face of fear. You can also choose to be prejudiced, judgmental, and opinionated. But if you do, your life will be controlled by other people's discrimination, condemnation, and narrow-mindedness.

You can choose to do just enough to get by and not fully contribute in your work or business, your home life, or in your relationships in general. You will then wonder why your life is boring, your work is drudgery or your business isn't growing, and you never seem to have any meaningful, heartfelt, win-win relationships.

Remember the law of ten-fold return? Whatever you give comes back to you ten times over. You can choose to recreate yourself by raising your own bar, looking for the positive in every experience, working with passion and purpose, eliminating struggle, and using your gifts and talents to make the world a better place.

You can choose to play the game of life with enthusiasm and vigor, displaying ethics and upholding your values, helping others to succeed, taking risks, being unafraid to fail, expressing yourself fully, and letting yourself shine.

You can choose to stand up for what you believe is just and risk being unpopular. You can decide to open your eyes to a bigger world around you, embrace the differences that make us unique and marvel at the similitude that binds us all together: our good fortune in being a part of the human family.

You can go whatever way you want in life. How you live your life is your choice—plain and simple.

When you choose to be better than your best, you'll uncover the courage and strength necessary to face the daily challenges, disappointments, and hardships on your road to success. When you choose to be better than your best, you'll reap the benefits of living life with vitality, having relationships that nurture, and the deep satisfaction of knowing you are changing the world for the better.

When you know who you really are, your experiences will be authentic. You will have more energy, and you'll be in awe at the beauty of the world. The air will smell cleaner, the grass will be greener, the sky will be bluer, people will be nicer, and food will taste better. Your job or business will be rewarding and not only life-sustaining but growing as you grow and become the best you can be every day.

When you keep your thoughts, words, and actions positive, success will not only stop at your door, it will roll at your feet!

Why Wait? Start Now!

Keep in mind the wisdom of Harriet Martineau, "You had better live your best and act your best and think your best today; for today is the sure preparation for tomorrow and all the other tomorrows that follow."

"When you choose to be better than your best, you'll uncover the courage and strength necessary to face the daily challenges, disappointments, and hardships on your road to success."

—Danny and Marie Lena

Who Are
Danny and Marie Lena?

Authors and dynamic professionals, Danny and Marie Lena are living examples of people practicing what they preach. As President and Director of PEP Programs, this dynamic husband and wife team has dedicated their lives to helping others recreate themselves. Married for over 19 years and working together for over 23, the Lenas' animated, inspirational presentations delight thousands of people annually.

As hosts of their own radio show on the Internet, Danny and Marie interview authors, luminaries, business leaders, and innovators worldwide to discover new ways to raise our own bar to create a happier, safer, more productive world. The Lenas have authored several books on personal safety and empowerment, as well as workbooks on personal success.

They are both karate black belts and gourmet cooks, and they live in Chicago, Illinois, with their five-pound Maltese puppy-dog, Tina.